The Mohave Rattlesnake

And How It Became An Urban Legend

Mike Cardwell

The Mohave Rattlesnake And How It Became An Urban Legend

Michael D. Cardwell

ISBN 978-1-938850-30-1

Copies available from:

ECO Publishing
4 Rattlesnake Canyon Road
Rodeo, New Mexico 88056
Telephone: (575) 557-5757; (575) 545-5307
FAX: (575) 557-7575
E-mail: desertmuseum@gmail.com

Design and Layout
Russ Gurley and Emory Schuett

Cover Design
Charles Smith

Images
Michael D. Cardwell unless otherwise attributed.

Printed in China.

Contents

Foreword

Upon reading this remarkably clear and complete book, I found myself a bit worried. After all, Mike Cardwell had asked me to write a Foreword and, having spent much of my life involved with venomous snakes, I naturally planned on gracing this page with some complementary nuggets of info not covered in the story. But I couldn't; I discovered that I had nothing to add to Mike's thorough and lucid account of the Mohave rattlesnake. Frankly, I learned a lot by reading it.

Surely, I thought, I can contribute something. But as I reviewed sections covering everything from life history to cultural importance, snakebite, fallacious beliefs, Internet hysteria, distribution, behavior, and ongoing research, I realized I was reading a careful and thorough story. While it lucidly explains just about everything that pertains to the Mohave rattlesnake, it is also filled with wisdom and common sense about rattlesnakes in general. And it is accessible; by that I mean it has been written in such a manner that one need not be a scientist to understand and enjoy this book.

Commonly suggested traits to identify rattlesnakes, like pupil shape and heat-sensitive facial pits, are far too small to be seen from a safe distance.

Then I realized that something did merit mention. Beneath this explanation of all things Mohave there is a love story. It began as a boy's interest and fascination with a snake and it deepened and endured, even when life carried him into other endeavors. In fact, Mike's career training, with emphasis on forensics, procedure, understanding human nature, and calmly injecting order into chaos…all of this influences and informs his approach to teaching us about the Mohave rattlesnake, about how to unravel its convoluted history, and how to find the truth behind myth and superstition.

Scientists are sometimes depicted as emotionless intellectuals, locked firmly in a secular world of exploration. Indeed, some fit into that category, but the best ones do not. Ironically, science is, at its core, an act of faith. Those who engage in science seek the truth, and thus believe that truth exists. And that brings us back to Mike's career training, which was to seek the truth about people and their doings. One cannot read this book without realizing that Mike cares about people as much as he cares about Mohave rattlesnakes. Throughout, he writes with tact and diplomacy. Rather than denigrate those whose beliefs about this snake are erroneous, Mike tries to understand their viewpoint while gently nudging the reader towards the truth. As much as he writes to correct the record about this snake, he also writes with firm desire to enrich the lives of people. So, there is a second love story hidden in this book.

I met Mike Cardwell not in the US but on the Amazon River in Peru, where he had come in search of reptiles and amphibians. We spent a delightful week getting to know the rainforest, the local culture, and each other. Then, as now, I was struck by the patience and understanding that he brought to the table. Over the nearly three decades since that time, on trips to Peru and the Brazilian frontier, I have come to know and respect this quiet, tenacious, thoughtful person as not only a friend, but also an inspiration. For me, this book is actually about Mike Cardwell. I see him on every page, seeking the truth, calmly confronting and unraveling mysteries, and motivated by a love of snakes and a love of people. It makes me smile.

William W. Lamar

Tyler, Texas
September, 2019

Acknowledgements

Many people and institutions have contributed to my ability to study and understand Mohave rattlesnakes. To anyone I may have omitted, I sincerely apologize. My original 40-month radiotelemetry study was primarily supported by Bill Hayes, Sean Bush, and others at Loma Linda University. Additionally, David Hardy, Sr. and Gordon Schuett were invaluable mentors. Many others have shared with me their unpublished data and observations of Mohave rattlesnakes, as well as field and surgical techniques, including Tracy Brown, Dale DeNardo, Eric Dugan, Marty Feldner, Matt Goode, Harry Greene, Bob Hansen, Erika Nowak, Randy Reiserer, Roger Repp, Emily Taylor, Wolfgang Wüster, and Giulia Zancolli.

William Degenhardt, Terry Johnson, Dennis Miller, Robert Murphy, Charlie Painter, Cecil Schwalbe, and Alan Tennant provided their recollections of data for previously published accounts. Jamie Kneitel, Ron Coleman, Winston Lancaster, Miles Roberts, and others at Cal State Sacramento encouraged and supported my work and assisted with data analysis. Access to museum material has been provided by Margi Dykens, Brad Hollingsworth, and Laura Williams (SDNHM); Roy McDiarmid, Steve Gotte, and James Poindexter II (USNM); Ned Gilmore (ANSP), Michelle Koo, Jim McGuire, and Carol Spencer (MVZ); Kent Beaman, Neftali Camacho and Greg Pauly (LACM); George Bradley (UAZ); Alan Resetar (FMNH); and Jens Vindum (CAS). HerpNET (www.herpnet.org) was an invaluable resource.

In addition to those mentioned above, other colleagues who have provided expert advice on various aspects of Mohave rattlesnake natural history, genetics, taxonomy and venom pharmacology include John Cadle, Jon Campbell, Rulon Clark, Andy Holycross, Larry Jones, Bill Lamar, Steve Mackessy, Dan Massey, William Mautz, Jude McNally, John Murphy, Bree Putman, Mark Riley and Robert Villa. John Fahey shared his historical knowledge and archival material regarding Bernard J. D. Irwin and Irwin's time at Fort Buchanan. Suggestions by Gordon Schuett, Marty Feldner, Hans-Werner Herrmann, and Wolfgang Wüster improved my Mohave rattlesnake chapter in *Rattlesnakes of Arizona* – upon which this book relies heavily. Sean Bush, MD, provided suggestions for the portions of this book dealing with medical issues relating to rattlesnake

After initially having trouble finding this telemetered Mohave rattlesnake one night, I finally detected a weak signal, only to discover him coiled inside an old steel food can that effectively shielded his radio signal from my antenna.

bites. Bill Lamar kindly provided the Foreword and his editorial comments greatly improved the manuscript.

Rulon Clark has allowed me to associate with his lab at San Diego State University, facilitating my studies being approved by the SDSU Institutional Animal Care and Use Committee – an essential detail for publishing in scholarly journals. Matt Goode at the University of Arizona has provided supplies and other invaluable support. My Mohave rattlesnake field studies have been made possible by permits issued by the Arizona Game and Fish Department, California Department of Fish and Wildlife, and the U.S. Bureau of Land Management. Consent to work on its property was also granted by Cemex Corporation.

Finally, I will be forever indebted to my wonderful wife Denise, who frequently accompanies me in the field and has graciously tolerated the expenditure of immense amounts of time and other resources on my herpetological endeavors over many years.

Preface

A participant at one of my recent rattlesnake programs asked me, "What's the difference between a Mohave rattlesnake and a Mohave green?" This book answers that question – and more. In the following pages, I summarize in non-technical language what biologists, toxicologists, physicians, and other experts know about Mohave rattlesnakes and how the mythical Mohave green compares to the real animal. More so than other rattlesnakes, exaggerated tales about Mohave rattlesnakes have produced a legendary reputation for this animal and a rather universal paranoia among residents in the American Southwest. In trying to educate folks about Mohave rattlesnakes over the years, I have been amazed and frustrated by the amount of folklore and unsubstantiated rumors that so many storytellers passionately swear to be fact. And these storytellers are too often educated people whom others assume to be credible, sometimes including physicians, game wardens, and even wildlife biologists who specialize in other areas of biology. It is particularly troubling when the news media gives life to these myths without consulting credible authorities.

Since about the age of eight, when my mother's cat brought a small kingsnake into our Los Angeles home, I have been fascinated by animals that others unreasonably fear. The kingsnake was not seriously injured, as I remember, and it lived in a terrarium in my bedroom for a long time thereafter. But two things are memorable after all these years: my complete fascination with the little animal and my bewilderment with my parents' trepidation over it. I do not recall ever having seen a snake before and I was mesmerized by this beautiful shy little creature that seemed to move so effortlessly, despite its lack of appendages.

My parents, Harvey and Bettie, were not phobic about snakes as are so many other people, despite their lack of familiarity. They apparently sensed, somehow, that the widespread fear most Americans harbor was probably exaggerated and they were able to put aside any misgivings when they saw my reaction. I have no idea how they determined it was not dangerous but they apparently made some inquiries, because we soon learned not only what kind it was but what it ate. It turns out that my mother was more afraid of mice than snakes but she soon brought home some small mice from a pet store. The kingsnake and I were happy. Well, I was happy… and the kingsnake was safe from the cat!

By the time we moved out of Los Angeles in 1963, I was thirteen years old and had a garage full of snakes, lizards, and assorted other creatures. We moved about a hundred miles northeast to Apple Valley, in the western Mohave Desert, which was home to a different assortment of reptiles than the foothills around Los Angeles. I soon learned that the most abundant snake in the area was the Mohave rattlesnake. Nearby rocky hills were full of southwestern speckled rattlesnakes and sidewinders were abundant in the flat desert a few miles away. But Mohaves were commonly encountered by friends and neighbors and it was these "Mohave greens" that were the subject of many crazy tales that seemed so implausible to me.

By high school, my interest in snakes, spiders, scorpions, bats, and the like – creatures I viewed as unreasonably feared by others – was becoming well known locally. In the relatively unregulated 1960s, I had accumulated a rather impressive collection of mostly local animals at our rural home, which attracted sporadic school field trips. On several occasions, a big yellow school bus waited in front of our house while I played tour guide and interpretive naturalist, having been allowed to take a half day off from school myself for the occasion. As my modest reputation grew, more people felt compelled to tell me their scary snake stories – usually involving Mohave greens. At the same time, I was getting to know this shy and interesting desert dweller and I was dismayed that so many people actually believed these small animals, weighing less than a pound, would initiate confrontations with creatures as large as humans.

Invariably each spring, the local newspaper would write a story about how people should be alert because the Mojave greens were out. The reporter usually quoted local "experts"– folks who had lived in the desert for decades and claimed to have "studied" Mojave greens. They spread crazy stories like, "The dreaded and lethal Mojave green rattlesnakes" produce "between 50 and 125 babies at one time" and are "taking over this area" (The Victorville Daily Press, 10 September 1995). In the same article, a local emergency room physician is quoted proclaiming as fact the urban legend that baby rattlesnakes inject more venom than adults. In 1996, a local "expert" claimed that Mojave greens had "steadily eaten or chased out other species of snakes since first showing up in the Kramer Junction area west of Barstow about 25 years ago" (The Victorville Daily Press, 25 May 1996). Then it was suggested that Mohave rattlesnake venom "can lie dormant in a person's system for years and can be unexpectedly reactivated by trauma" later in life (The Victorville Daily Press, 7 May 1998). And on and on!

Years later, after I had established a reputation as a credible authority on rattlesnakes and other desert creatures – and even writing a regular desert wildlife column for the same newspaper, new reporters would occasionally interview the old self-proclaimed "experts" and print another sensational story. And I would go into damage-control mode again, educating another journalist in the process.

Mohave rattlesnakes are often described as aggressive, deadly, and even angry. They are sometimes said to chase people. Some claim that they are not ordinary rattlesnakes, or not rattlesnakes at all. Some swear they have no rattles, that antivenom is useless against their bites, or that they are some kind of recent hybrid. Because erroneous information about rattlesnakes is so common, it is important for me to provide you with trustworthy references (found in the back of this book) where you can look up much of the information I will present in the pages that follow.

I went through high school and two years of college majoring in math and science. But when a couple of older friends were unable to find jobs as biologists after graduation, I began to realize that such jobs were scarce in 1970. At the same time, I was volunteering with the local sheriff's search and rescue unit and was soon recruited to join the San Bernardino County Sheriff's Department.

I worked for SBSD from 1972 until 2004, eventually rising to be chief of the Specialized Operations Bureau. During my law enforcement career, I was fortunate enough to get to work all the assignments that Hollywood makes movies about – homicide, narcotics, SWAT, career criminals, public corruption and even counterterrorism. Less sensational assignments included patrol, custody (i.e., jail – a joy unique to sheriff's departments) and internal criminal investigations. Although I changed my early major course of study to administration of justice, I never lost my fascination with venomous creatures. I eventually tried to finish my undergraduate degree in biology but found that the duties of my day job did not allow the commitment necessary for the five-unit lab classes and I had to settle for an AS degree in math and science – temporarily.

The heart of being a credible expert in any scientific topic is reading the relevant literature published in peer-reviewed scholarly journals, both past and current. I will be forever indebted to my high school biology instructor, David Browne, who taught me the scientific method and how to search the scientific literature at UC Riverside's old Bio-Ag Library. As a result of those early but invaluable lessons, I was able to stay abreast of research during my law enforcement career on venomous animals and the injuries they cause, spending much of my spare time in the libraries at UC Riverside and Loma Linda University. And over time, my speaking invitations progressed from school kids and service clubs to audiences like utility company employees, park rangers, and paramedics. Although my early reputation was for expertise on rattlesnakes, frequent questions about scorpions, spiders, and other creatures, as well as first aid, prompted me to expand my studies into those areas, as well.

Around 1980, I got serious about photography. I eventually published some wildlife photos and won some awards, but the real value of this effort was the addition of my own stunning images to my lectures on venomous bites and stings. The combination of great photography with my growing reputation for accurate information really boosted the popularity of my presentations.

In 1985, I joined the Wilderness Medical Society and was eventually invited to speak at several of the annual WMS conferences. Although I had become accustomed to lecturing about venomous snakes and snakebite to paramedics and a few physicians locally, it was quite intimidating to stand before an auditorium full of wilderness medicine specialists, many of whom were physicians, and lecture to them about my topic. But their thoughtful questions and kind compliments quickly bolstered my confidence. I found that, except for a few envenomation specialists, they were largely as naïve as others about venomous creatures!

In April 1994, the death of a local high school athletic coach, injured while he worked in his yard a few miles from my Apple Valley home, was initially attributed to baby Mohave rattlesnakes by the local news media, although his reported signs and symptoms were textbook acute allergic reaction and inconsistent with snakebite. It was later determined that he had a pre-existing allergy to insect stings and his yard was full of harvester ants. Before his death, he was transferred to Loma Linda University Medical Center and, in the wake of this tragedy, I became acquainted with a young resident emergency medicine physician named Sean Bush. Like the rest of us, Sean had been a reptile enthusiast as a boy and he soon made his mark in emergency medicine as an internationally-respected envenomation expert.

In 1996, Dr. Bill Hayes arrived at Loma Linda University as an associate professor in the Life Sciences Department. Bill had done his doctoral dissertation research on how much venom rattlesnakes inject during predatory strikes and he had a passion for learning more about these creatures. Bill, Sean, and I became great friends and the combination of new research into the snakes' biology and behavior by Bill and his graduate students combined with Sean's clinical experience and experimental efforts regarding snakebite first aid and treatment proved to be a potent combination for expanding our understanding of rattlesnakes and their bites. Sean and Bill embraced me as a research colleague, despite my lack of official affiliation with the university, and included me in their efforts. They also supported my own field studies, including equipment, software, and surgical supplies for my first long-term radiotelemetry study of wild Mohave rattlesnakes (2001–2004). The three of

Mohave rattlesnake in full defensive display. Rather than "angry" or "aggressive," as such rattlesnakes are usually described, this animal is behaving defensively, trying to look and sound as threatening and dangerous as possible. It wants nothing to do with an organism as large as a human. The colored paint in the rattle is a method of marking individual rattlesnakes for visual identification during a field study.

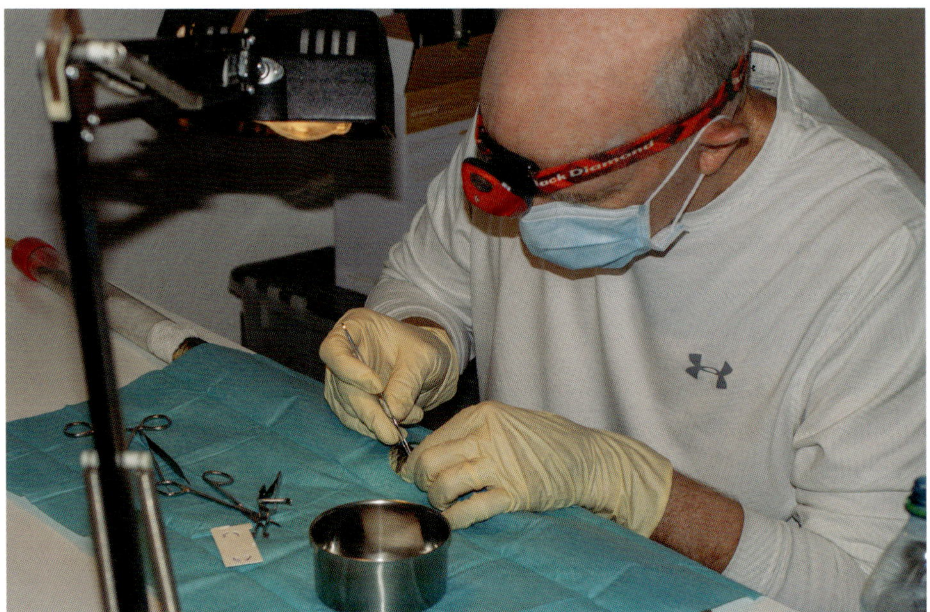

I surgically implant radio transmitters in the abdominal cavities of rattlesnakes, allowing them to be located at any time and their behavior studied. Before miniature long-lasting surgically-implantable transmitters became available, it was impossible to effectively study cryptic free-ranging animals like rattlesnakes. Photo by Denise Garland.

us, plus Kent Beaman of the Los Angeles County Natural History Museum, eventually organized and hosted the initial Biology of the Rattlesnakes symposium at Loma Linda University (15–18 January 2005), followed by the 600-page reference book *The Biology of Rattlesnakes* (2008, LLU Press), co-edited by the four of us and containing the peer-reviewed research of more than ninety authors.

Since it is not practical to put a collar or other external package on a snake, field studies require that small radio transmitters be surgically implanted inside the snakes' abdomens. I will be forever indebted to several other herpetologists who coached me on what equipment to use and how to implant the transmitters. In particular, the late Dr. David Hardy Sr., a retired Tucson anesthesiologist who had extensive experience radio-tracking rattlesnakes and who had published technical articles on successful anesthesia and transmitter surgery, provided an instructional video of the procedure and tirelessly answered my questions. With the help of Bill Hayes, my transmitter surgery protocol and field study was approved by Loma Linda University's Animal Research Committee – an essential detail to obtain permits and for publication of my findings in scholarly journals. The California Department of Fish and Wildlife granted the necessary scientific collecting permits for my early field work.

Sean Bush and I implanted my first transmitter in a Mohave rattlesnake in Sean's garage in August 2001. I have since performed more than 200 transmitter surgeries myself and taught the procedure to several other herpetologists. My first Mohave rattlesnake field study continued for 40 months, until the snakes went down for the winter in November 2004. I moved to Sacramento the same month but returned the following April to remove the remaining transmitters. During the study, I collected data at more than 3,700 close encounters with 85 Mohave rattlesnakes and my field experiences were prominently featured in Animal Planet's Venom ER television series (2004). I have since presented findings from that study at various scientific meetings around the United States and Canada, as well as publishing several manuscripts in peer-reviewed journals and books, with more in the works.

I returned to school after retirement from law enforcement and found that many of my previous math and science classes would have to be repeated. Nonetheless, I earned my Bachelor of Science in Biology (graduating cum laude) at California State University Sacramento in 2010, followed by a Master of Science degree in Ecology, Evolution, and Conservation in 2013, also from CSUS. For the master's degree, my thesis committee allowed me to use my Mohave rattlesnake data to compare rattlesnake behavior during the drought year 2002 with corresponding behavior during 2003 and 2004, when precipitation returned to normal or above normal. As a result, I produced "Behavioral Changes by Mohave Rattlesnakes (*Crotalus scutulatus*) in Response to Drought", with some interesting findings I will discuss later (Cardwell, 2013).

As part of my master's degree studies, I set out to untangle the confused record of the original description of the Mohave rattlesnake. That successful endeavor involved collaboration with colleagues at the Smithsonian Institution and the Academy of Natural Sciences of Philadelphia and resulted in a publication entitled "Type specimens of *Crotalus scutulatus* (Chordata: Reptilia: Squamata: Viperidae) re-examined, with new evidence after more than a century of confusion" in the Proceedings of the Biological Society of Washington (Cardwell et al., 2013). In addition to other recent projects, including serving on a panel of subject matter experts who revised the treatment guidelines for North American pitviper bites (Kanaan et al., 2015) and co-authoring the chapter on North American reptile bites for the seventh edition of Paul Auerbach's *Wilderness Medicine* (Norris, Bush, and Cardwell, 2015), I was honored to be invited by the lead editor, Dr. Gordon Schuett, to write the Mohave rattlesnake chapter for a new reference book titled *Rattlesnakes of Arizona*, published in 2016 by ECO Publishing in Rodeo, New Mexico.

Rattlesnakes of Arizona is a wonderful two-volume compilation of cutting-edge rattlesnake lore by the current experts on each of the 15 kinds of rattlesnakes found in the Grand Canyon State, plus equally notable chapters on such topics as venom evolution, the rattle, genetic analyses, conservation and much more. While drafting the Mohave rattlesnake account for *ROA*, I dug deeply into issues like the maximum documented length, the species' evolutionary origin, habitat preferences, and evidence of wild hybridization, to name a few. My research for *Rattlesnakes of Arizona* was not restricted to Arizona and this book benefits extensively from that effort. In particular, I thank Gordon Schuett and *ROA* publisher Bob Ashley (ECO Publishing) for permission to use my Mohave rattlesnake account from *ROA* as the basis for this book.

In 2017, Denise and I relocated to Tucson – which, combined with adjacent northern Mexico, is the biodiversity hotspot for rattlesnakes. South-central Arizona also contains the most dramatic and perplexing geographic variation in Mohave rattlesnake venom, which interests me tremendously. With support from Dr. Rulon Clark and San Diego State University, plus cooperation and permits from the Arizona Department of Game and Fish and the U.S. Bureau of Land Management, I launched my second radiotelemetry study of wild Mohave rattlesnakes in southern Arizona in 2018.

I hope you enjoy the book. My goal is not to create rattlesnake lovers but, rather, to reduce your fear of rattlesnakes in general and Mohave rattlesnakes in particular. Replacing sensational myths with well-documented information will allow you to more fully enjoy the outdoors and view an occasional rattlesnake encounter as an exciting and interesting experience – from a safe distance!

Mike Cardwell

Tucson, Arizona
April 2019

Introduction

In the following pages, I have summarized what biologists, toxicologists, and emergency medicine experts know about Mohave rattlesnakes, particularly topics about which people most frequently ask. Near the end, I have included more generalized rattlesnake lore, especially myths and urban legends about rattlesnakes in general. Finally, I have explained how to avoid rattlesnake bites and what snakebite experts suggest you do for someone who is bitten.

WHAT'S IN THE BOOK?

Mohave rattlesnakes have various names in different parts of the American Southwest. I cover those names in the first chapter, including what we know about the proper spelling of Mohave (Mojave?). I also discuss the scientific name and what I believe Robert Kennicott had in mind when he named the species more than 150 years ago.

Chapter 2 contains details about the characteristic appearance of Mohave rattlesnakes and their distribution in the United States. In some cases, Mohaves and other species look remarkably alike and Mohave rattlesnake look-alikes are found in many places where actual Mohaves are absent. In Chapter 3, you will find the specific differences between Mohave rattlesnakes and other species with which they are sometimes confused and how to tell them apart.

A favorite claim of those who know only the "Mohave green" folklore has been that they are a recent hybrid, without the typical biological history of other organisms. Despite lots of genetic evidence and some corresponding fossils, this myth was bolstered by lack of a "type specimen" – the preserved museum animal used for the original scientific description of a species. That changed in 2013 when I, along with colleagues at the Smithsonian Institution's National Museum of Natural History and the Academy of Natural Sciences of Philadelphia, discovered a 100-year-old specimen tagging error. We also found that the correct type specimen had been discovered more than 80 years ago by the foremost rattlesnake expert of the twentieth century, only to be apparently overlooked in later years and never published. Follow this biological cold case in Chapter 4.

Pitviper venoms are some of the most complex and variable animal toxins in nature. This is no less true of Mohave rattlesnake venom, which has been the subject of intense research for fifty years. As a result, Mohaves are considered to be the deadliest of North American rattlesnakes by almost everyone, including many physicians and herpetologists. Most well-respected publications with individual species accounts, including field guides and medical references, warn of the extraordinary danger posed by Mohave rattlesnakes. I describe where this idea originated, what researchers who study such things have found, and why I'd rather be bitten by a Mohave than almost any other North American rattlesnake. Mohave rattlesnakes are, indeed, the deadliest rattlesnake – if you're a lab mouse! I explain why in Chapter 5 as well as discussing what science tells us about Mohave rattlesnake venom – which may be just as strange as the folklore.

Hybridization is often mentioned by desert residents concerned about Mohave greens and potential hybrids are of great interest to biologists and toxicologists, as well. Rattlesnakes with odd patterns and colors have been encountered occasionally ever since early biologists began exploring North America. Yet only recently have advances in molecular biology allowed scientists to compare individual snakes at the genetic level to determine if they possess genes from more than one species. New information is announced constantly in journals and at scientific meetings. In Chapter 6, I present what we know about hybridization as this book goes to print and where geneticists think the evidence points.

I discuss the Mohave rattlesnake's population status in an era of habitat destruction, urbanization and a warming climate in Chapter 7. Read this chapter to find out which state legally protects America's most misunderstood rattlesnake.

Habits and behavior of wild Mohave rattlesnakes are summarized in Chapter 8. Radiotelemetry has opened a window into the private lives of rattlesnakes and we are beginning to understand the seasonal habits, reproductive behavior and foraging strategy of many species. In this chapter, I discuss what we know about how Mohave rattlesnakes live, based largely on my pioneering 2001–2004 radiotelemetry study and new on-going studies as I write. And while we expect to find Mohaves living in deserts, they also live in some non-desert habitats like grasslands and pinion-juniper woodlands. Read Chapter 8 to learn about the private lives of Mohave rattlesnakes.

The effects of Mohave rattlesnake bites are discussed in Chapter 9, including the difference between neurotoxic venom-A bites and tissue-destroying venom-B bites.

In Chapter 10, I list the most common Mohave green myths and describe how Mohave rattlesnakes have been treated in the news media, often publishing erroneous information – sometimes quoted from folks who should know better. The problem here is that many people tend to believe – or at least repeat – such stories, which soon take on a life of their own. Read Chapter 10 to find out about the one snake in fifty years that "attacked" me and why it happened. Then in Chapter 11, I discuss Internet hoaxes, where anyone can reach millions of people instantly with crazy claims.

Chapter 12 discusses other rattlesnake myths in general, most of which are applied to Mohaves too. Some are extraordinarily widespread and cry out for a proper explanation. For example, who hasn't heard that baby rattlesnakes are more dangerous than adults? You must read Chapter 12!

You will learn how rattlesnake bites happen in Chapter 13 and how to avoid the two human behaviors that produce bites. Then, in Chapter 14, I explain the proper first aid for rattlesnake bites, as recommended by the Wilderness Medical Society. Finally, I cover what to expect when you reach the emergency room, as well as a brief discussion of antivenom and historic first aid techniques. Learn what snakebite physicians suggest in Chapter 14.

FINDING AND READING REFERENCES CITED IN THIS BOOK

This book is full of references where you can look up independent sources for certain information and where you can often find additional material. Much of my expertise comes from more than fifty years of collecting, keeping, and studying rattlesnakes – especially Mohave rattlesnakes. Like other wildlife biologists, I mostly study living – and often wild – animals, while physiologists, taxonomists, biochemists, toxinologists, geneticists, paleontologists and certain emergency medicine professionals study related areas like a species' origin and evolution, natural history, venom components and effects, and first aid and treatment for bites. Scientists and physicians publish their research in technical journals and books that require their writings and conclusions to be reviewed, usually anonymously, by other experts in the field, as well as by an editorial staff before publication. This process, called "peer-review," is designed to guard against publication of unsubstantiated findings and conclusions. Although not foolproof in the short term, it works pretty well – especially over time.

I have authored and co-authored many such peer-reviewed articles, peer-reviewed many manuscripts by other scientists and physicians, and served as an editor for a 600-page peer-reviewed book containing the work of 90 researchers (*The Biology of Rattlesnakes*, 2008, Loma Linda University Press). I can tell you that virtually no manuscript makes it through the review process without at least answering questions from reviewers and editors, adding additional explanation or even having to completely re-write the paper. Some manuscripts are simply rejected. Furthermore, an important part of the scientific process is describing experimental and observational methods in enough detail that other researchers can repeat the work. Finally, scientists are trained to be a skeptical bunch and they savor the opportunity to point out flaws in each other's work or even disprove a colleague's conclusions entirely.

My point is that such published research, while generally reliable, is not readily available in most public libraries or even online, except in summary or "abstract" form. Yet those kinds of publications are precisely what I will cite for many of the references in this book because they are written by the experts on a specific topic and critiqued by other experts before publication. My comments on rattlesnakes in the news media and internet hoaxes (Chapters 10 and 11) demonstrate why we should be very skeptical about what we read and hear from such sources.

Abstracts, while providing only a summary of scientists' findings, are available for most journal articles by searching for the reference online. But in some cases, the information for which I have cited an article may not have been the primary focus of the research and, thus, is not mentioned in the abstract. In other cases, an article may be a review of multiple previous research efforts on a particular topic. At the time of this writing, Google Scholar® is a free and easy-to-use search engine for scientific papers. In this digital age, many journals are now available online and some are only online (i.e., there is no paper edition). In the Literature Cited section at the end of this book, you will find the abbreviation "doi:" at the end of some references, followed by an alphanumeric "address" that will take you directly to the digital article when entered into your browser.

For those interested in looking at the complete version of a scientific article (without purchasing it online), a visit to a university library is usually in order. Most university libraries have a few "public" computers where you may be able to download a PDF copy or at least find the call number for the journal so you can retrieve the appropriate issue from the shelves. A librarian can assist with this process.

Literature is cited in the book by the lead author's last name and the year of publication; for example: (Kennicott, 1861). If there are two authors, both last names are used. If more than two authors, the reference is cited with the lead author's last name followed by the abbreviation "et al." meaning "and others." If a specific page is referenced, it follows the year, separated by a colon. Therefore, (Kanaan, et al., 2015:478) refers to page 478 in an article published in 2015 by Kanaan and more than one additional author. If the author's name(s) are part of a sentence, the year of publication may stand alone in parentheses. In any case, the entire citation can then be found in the Literature Cited section in the back of this book.

Scientific papers are full of intimidating terms, acronyms, and other jargon – even for scientists. The good news is that this technical language is mostly confined to the "Methods" and "Results" sections of the papers, which there is little need to understand unless you are interested in critiquing or repeating the work. However, the "Introduction" will usually provide a lot of useful background information, including previous related findings and publications, and the "Discussion" and/or "Conclusions" sections will provide more readable explanations of the authors' interpretation of their results.

Metric Measurements

Scientific papers are also full of metric measurements and statistics, so I want to give you a very brief explanation of both. So that research can be easily shared and understood around the world, scientists everywhere use standardized units of measure called SI units (short for System International d'Unités). SI units include meters (and multiples like millimeters, centimeters, and kilometers) for length and kilograms (including milligrams, grams, etc.) for weight or "mass." Of course, there are other units for things like temperature, area, volume, force, and all manner of measurable phenomenon. Tables and formulas to convert these units to inches, ounces, and other familiar measures are easily available online and in dictionaries.

Statistical Analyses

Statistics are now routinely reported in scientific papers, so here is the most important point to remember about statistical data: The most common purpose of reporting statistical results is to measure the mathematical probability that an observed result is "real" and not due to chance. While there are many complex methods to compute this probability (usually reported as the p-value or P-value), the accepted convention in science is that a result should be discounted if the mathematical probability that it is due to chance (i.e., accident or coincidence) is 5% or greater, expressed as $p \geq 0.05$ (read as "p is greater than or equal to 5%"). Therefore, scientists need a p-value of less than 5% ($p < 0.05$ or "p is less than 5%") to consider their results meaningful and statistically "significant."

For example, can we conclude that there is something wrong with a coin if we flip it three times and it comes up heads every time? Well, no, because the probability that the result is simply a coincidence is 12.5% ($p = 0.125$), well over 5% (I'll spare you from the math). This example suffers from a small sample size (in this case, the sample size is three; we flipped the coin only three times) and that's a common problem with making meaningful conclusions from some research. But if we increase the sample size, say to 5 (i.e., we flip the coin five times), and all flips produce heads, the result becomes "significant" at $p = 0.031$ (the chance of the result being merely a coincidence is only 3.1%). If we flip ten times and still get all heads, $p = 0.00098$, which is usually reported as $p < 0.001$ (i.e., the probability of the result being due to chance is less than one tenth of one percent or less than one in a thousand), so the likelihood that there is a real problem with the coin is very high. But if we get eight heads out of ten flips, the probability that there is something wrong with the coin is still considered significant at $p = 0.044$ (less than 0.05) but much less convincing than $p < 0.001$. If we get only seven heads out of ten flips, the result is not considered significant at $p = 0.117$ (beyond the threshold of 0.05). I hope you get the idea.

Scientific Skepticism

An important concept to understand here, as when considering all scientific results, is that a tiny p-value like $p = 0.00098$ does not prove there is something wrong with the coin; it only indicates that the likelihood of the result being due to chance alone is so small as to render that conclusion unreasonable – but the chance is not zero. Biologists are trained that they can never prove anything and there is always room for some doubt. Unlike many discoveries in physics and chemistry, few concepts in the life sciences can be proven with mathematical equations. Thus, an apparently valid concept in biology only gains acceptance over time as it survives repeated attempts to disprove it. This idea is often misunderstood – or intentionally misrepresented – by those who seek to discredit science for financial, political, or religious purposes.

1 What's in a Name?

Animal names are generally divided into two categories: "common" or "English" names – those used by people who live in or otherwise frequent the area where the critter occurs, and "scientific" or "Latin" names used by biologists and other scientists. Interestingly, both can vary. Common names tend to vary between geographic areas and often between cultures. Scientific names vary over time, as scientists refine their ideas about which organisms are most closely related and share a recent common ancestor.

COMMON ENGLISH NAMES

Common names are localized terms used to identify local animals. For the most part, they are not regulated and often mean different things to different people. Local folks may have several names for the same animal and the same name is often used for different organisms in various parts of the country. For example, the animal called "timber rattlesnake" in the Appalachian Mountains of the northeastern United States is a completely different species than the rattlesnake called by the same name in the San Gabriel and San Bernardino Mountains of southern California. And many folks call any rattlesnake with large dorsal blotches "diamondback," even though many different species share this trait. Some biologists discourage any use of common names but others point out that they serve a purpose, especially if applied with consistency, while we all try to stay abreast of constant changes in the scientific names – mostly based on new genetic analyses.

To that end, efforts to standardize common names for reptiles and amphibians in the United States and Canada have been undertaken since at least 1956 (Conant et al., 1956). In 2000, the first standardized list of common and scientific names endorsed by the three major North American herpetological societies – the Society for the Study of Amphibians and Reptiles, the American Society of Ichthyologists and Herpetologists, and the Herpetologists' League – was published (Crother, 2000). Beginning with the seventh edition (Crother, 2012), the names have been additionally sanctioned by Partners in Amphibian and Reptile Conservation and various Canadian herpetological organizations. The frequency of recent published updates and revisions (Crother, 2003, 2008, 2012, 2017) is a testament to the pace at which geneticists and taxonomists are renaming the animals.

The Mojave Desert is characterized by two species of tree yuccas: the Joshua Tree (*Yucca brevifolia*) and the Mojave yucca (*Y. schidigera*). This area in San Bernardino County, California, near the boundary with Clark County, Nevada, is home to a healthy population of Mohave rattlesnakes.

The standardized list published in 2000 named the Mohave rattlesnake found in the United States and northern Mexico (*Crotalus scutulatus scutulatus*) "Mojave Green Rattlesnake" (Crother, 2000). However, subsequent editions have called the same animal "Northern Mohave Rattlesnake" (Crother, 2003, 2008, 2012 2017), referring to its northern distribution relative to a closely-related animal, the Huamantlan rattlesnake (*Crotalus scutulatus salvini*) found in a comparatively tiny area deep in central mainland Mexico. Northern Mohave rattlesnakes are common animals in the Mohave Desert and that is presumably the genesis of their common name, although the vast majority of their distribution lies in the Sonoran and Chihuahuan Deserts, mostly south of the U. S. border.

Mohave or Mojave

The spelling of Mohave with an "h" or a "j" has been debated in many circles for years (summarized by Cardwell, 2016 and Jones, 2016). In my experience, it is most often spelled with a "j" (e.g., Mojave Indian Tribe). Regarding the rattlesnake, the great 20th century rattlesnake authority Laurence Klauber first spelled Mojave rattlesnake with a "j" but used both spellings in the same paper when referring to the desert (Klauber, 1930) and he went on to use both spellings seemingly interchangeably in later publications. More recently, well-known Arizona herpetologist Charles Lowe wrote in the preface to *The Venomous Reptiles of Arizona* that "Mohave" is the correct spelling, with the j-version having been "perpetrated by misguided Gringos of long ago" (Lowe et al., 1986:ix). This opinion was cited by Brian Crother and his nomenclature committee when they first designated "Northern Mohave Rattlesnake" as the standardized common name (Crother et al., 2003). Other authors (Campbell and Lamar, 2004:15 & 581; and Stewart, 1994:55) quoted Jaeger (1957), who asserted that "Mohave" is derived from the Native American word *hamakhava*, referring to the steep pointed mountains or "needles" on the east side of the Colorado River near the present-day town of Needles.

However, an extensive investigation of the etymology by Lorraine Sherer (Sherer, 1967) reveals that the English word was likely the attempt by early white explorers to pronounce, and then write down, the traditional name of the Indian tribe encountered along the Colorado River, beginning in 1826. Modern Mojave Indians formally adopted the English "Mojave" with a "j" in 1957 but their traditional tribal name has always been *Aha macave* (translation: people who live along the water), which white men had trouble pronouncing. According to Sherer (1967), while modern Mojave Indians understand and accept the various attempts to spell their traditional name in English, the word *hamakhava* is unknown to today's tribal members (circa 1967) and they

These Hohokam petroglyphs, created 550-1,550 years ago, are believed to represent bighorn sheep above and a rattlesnake below. They are located on Signal Hill within Saguaro National Park West near Tucson, Arizona.

dispute its interpretation as "three mountains" or anything similar. Sherer (1967) found that "Mohave" first appeared, spelled with an "h," in the writings of Kit Carson in 1829–30 and is not recorded with a "j" until 1854.

Given this history, it is difficult to argue that either spelling is wrong. I use Mohave because that is the form adopted by the professional societies to which I belong but I have stopped suggesting that the j-version is incorrect. Beginning in 2008, Crother and his committee of nomenclature experts have come to a similar conclusion. Citing "linguistic experts on Native American languages," they state that either spelling is correct but using the "j" or "h" is based on whether the context is Spanish or English, respectively (Crother, 2008, 2012, 2017). As a result, they have continued to use the h-spelling for the standardized English rattlesnake name.

You will find, however, that I spell "Mojave toxin" with a "j" in the following pages because that was the spelling used by the authors (Bieber et al., 1975) who first described and named the potent neurotoxin found in the venom of many Mohave rattlesnakes.

Local Informal Names

Of course, folks call Mohave rattlesnakes by many other local names. "Mohave green" is very common and refers to the pronounced greenish coloration of most – but not all – populations of Mohave rattlesnakes (e.g.,

Crother, 2000; Stebbins, 1985, 2003). Mohave green is also the name most commonly associated with the rich but unfortunate mythology that exaggerates the danger posed by Mohave rattlesnakes. "Coontail" rattlesnake is a reference to the black and white ringed tail of many Mohaves, although the widely distributed western diamond-backed rattlesnake (*Crotalus atrox*) and southern California's red diamond rattlesnake (*Crotalus ruber*) share this distinctive trait. "Diamondback" or "desert diamondback" refers to the row of large overlapping diamond-shaped dorsal blotches, which is a character shared by many rattlesnake species.

LATIN OR "LATINIZED" SCIENTIFIC NAMES

Because I am referring you to technical papers in scientific and medical journals, I need to give you some basic information about how to interpret scientific names.

Scientific names used by biologists consist of a Latinized genus and species but such names are frequently changed as either new genetic evidence is discovered regarding which organisms are most closely related or taxonomists decide that previous naming efforts have not followed accepted naming rules. Scientific name changes have become more frequent as genetic analysis has become easier and more affordable. Scientific names are part of a standardized naming convention established nearly 300 years ago, with modern additions and amendments critiqued via the peer-review process (discussed in the Introduction).

The standardized scientific naming system is supposed to serve the same purpose as standardized units for length, mass, and volume – one name by which biologists world-wide can identify a species. In this system, plants and animals have been traditionally grouped according to similarity, starting with widely-shared traits like backbones, to increasingly specific characters. At the specific end of this system is what we call a "binomial," which literally means "two names." Binomials consist of a genus name and a specific epithet, both of which are either Latin terms or Latinized names or words from other (often Greek) languages. When Latin or Greek words are used, they usually describe some trait of the organism. Latinized words from other languages are often invented to honor a location, the person who discovered the first specimen, or to honor a prominent biologist, explorer, or other person. Taken together, the genus and specific epithet make up the species name, which is always italicized in print. For Mohave rattlesnakes, this binomial is *Crotalus scutulatus*. The genus is always capitalized and the specific epithet always begins with a lower case letter.

In more formal citations, the author and year of the species' description is added to the genus and species. For example: "*Crotalus atrox* Baird and Girard 1853" indicates that *Crotalus atrox* (the western diamond-backed rattlesnake) was originally described by Baird and Girard in 1853 and the Latin name has not been changed. However, if you find the author and year in parentheses, it means that the currently-accepted name is not the original name. Example: "*Crotalus scutulatus* (Kennicott 1861)" indicates that the species we now call *Crotalus scutulatus* was originally described by Kennicott in 1861 but the parentheses tells us that *Crotalus scutulatus* is not the name Kennicott originally used. Notwithstanding this naming convention, the parentheses are frequently eliminated in many publications. (Trivia answer: Kennicott originally called the Mohave rattlesnake "*Caudisona scutulata*" in his 1861 description.)

Prior to the ability to analyze and compare DNA, classification decisions were based largely or exclusively on an organism's morphology – its structure and appearance. Naming decisions based on morphology, when made carefully and based on thoughtful study of the organisms involved, have often been validated by later genetic analyses. However, in other cases, molecular analyses have revealed ancestral relationships that were not apparent from studies of structure and appearance alone. These efforts usually result in reclassification of the organism, sometimes with two species being merged into one, while in other cases, groups of organisms long considered to be the same species are separated. Whether existing species are split apart or lumped together, scientific names are inevitably changed.

As part of this process, it has been common for a very long time to describe and name geographic races or "subspecies" within a species. These are usually populations that look different but are believed to be the same species – usually meaning that they can reproduce successfully with one another. In the case of Mohave rattlesnakes, there are currently two recognized subspecies: *Crotalus scutulatus scutulatus*, the original Arizona animal described more than 150 years ago (Kennicott, 1861; Cardwell et al., 2013), and *Crotalus scutulatus salvini*, the Huamantlan rattlesnake of central mainland Mexico described by Gloyd (1940).

If you are not clear on exactly what a species is and whether apparently closely related populations are different species or just subspecies, don't worry – you are not alone! Biologists debate these definitions passionately – and not always amicably. While molecular analyses have answered many questions about how closely various organisms are related, this new discipline has also raised new questions about how species are defined. These issues remain unsettled and are beyond the scope of this book. For those interested, an online search for "species defined" will yield plenty of additional information.

The person who originally describes a genus or species gets to select the name. In the case of *Crotalus scutulatus*, the name is descriptive, rather than honoring a place or person. The genus *Crotalus* was created more than 260 years ago and is derived from the Greek word *krotalon*, which refers to a castanet or noise-making device used by dancers. *Crotalus* includes most of the rattlesnakes; the only exceptions being the few species with large plates on top of the head belonging to the genus *Sistrurus*. Robert Kennicott did not explain his choice of *scutulata* (later changed to *scutulatus* by Edward Cope in 1875) for the specific epithet when he wrote his original description. But, according to Latin scholars, *scutulata* is a feminine Latin noun meaning "checked garment" and *scutulatus* is a masculine Latin adjective describing something shaped like a "diamond" or "lozenge" (Marchant and Charles, 1957). While it is easy to jump to the conclusion that the term is intended to describe the diamond-shaped dorsal markings, that interpretation makes little sense to me because it is not unique to this species. Rather, I agree with Klauber (1930) that Kennicott was referring to the unique "large flat plates" (Kennicott, 1861) on top of the Mohave rattlesnake's head when he described it.

After Howard Gloyd described the Mexican subspecies *Crotalus scutulatus salvini* in 1940, the original animal became known as *Crotalus scutulatus scutulatus*. Such redundant names identify the "nominate" race (i.e., the form that was described first, giving the species its name). Currently, genetic evidence suggests that *Crotalus scutulatus salvini* is likely a distinct species from *Crotalus scutulatus scutulatus* (Schield et al., 2018). If this southern race is eventually elevated to full species status, its name will almost certainly become *Crotalus salvini* and *Crotalus scutulatus* will, once again, refer only to the "Northern" Mohave rattlesnake. Again, if this sounds confusing, you are in good company!

A typical Mohave rattlesnake (*Crotalus scutulatus*) from San Bernardino County, California.

Description and Distribution 2

DESCRIPTION

Length

Mohave rattlesnakes are medium-sized rattlesnakes, with animals measuring over 40 inches long (excluding rattle) being uncommon today. From a data set of hundreds of Mohave rattlesnakes sampled in the early 1900s when large rattlesnakes were more common than today, Laurence Klauber (1972) described the total length (body + tail without rattle) of Mohaves as: average newborn = 10.4 inches, smallest pregnant female = 24.8 inches, and the largest Mohave rattlesnake he measured (male) = 48.5 inches.

When I examined Klauber's 528 handwritten Mohave rattlesnake data sheets archived at the San Diego Natural History Museum, I found the longest female in Klauber's datasheets (specimen no. CAS63894) to be 36.3 inches. I later examined this huge female at the California Academy of Sciences and was allowed to dissect her tail to verify her sex. Klauber's data sheets also contained records of two males that measured 44.7 inches. Interestingly, the longest female and one of these large males (specimen no. CAS63895) were part of the same shipment of 18 rattlesnakes from Hillside in Yavapai County, Arizona, sent to the California Academy of Sciences by Santa Fe Railroad workers in September 1930. The other 44.7-inch male is in the American Museum of Natural History collection (specimen no. AMNH27370) with only "Arizona" listed as its origin.

Klauber recorded only one Mohave rattlesnake longer than 44.7 inches: a 45.0-inch male (specimen no. SDSNH37635) in the collection of the San Diego Natural History Museum. The museum's catalogue indicates that SDSNH37635 was collected on 4 July 1946, 27 miles southwest of Sonoyta, which is located in the Mexican state of Sonora, just south of the Arizona border. Although Klauber (1972) listed "1,231 mm" (48.5 inches) as the longest Mohave rattlesnake he had examined, I found no record longer than 1,143 mm (45.0 inches) among his archived data sheets.

As in most rattlesnakes, male Mohave rattlesnakes attain greater lengths than females. Many previous authors have cited Tennant (1984) as reporting the longest Mohave rattlesnake on record: a Brewster County, Texas, male that measured "just over 54 inches." But Tennant told me in 2012 that he

A typically marked and colored Mohave rattlesnake.

worries that this animal might have been a misidentified western diamondback and he says he would omit this account if he were to revise his 1984 book. Although Tennant believes that this animal may have been preserved, I have tried unsuccessfully to find it in an institutional collection.

Writing of Arizona animals, Lowe, Schwalbe and Johnson (1986) described most of the large Mohave rattlesnakes encountered as being "three-footers" and weighing "about a pound," with "4.3 ft" as the maximum length. Neither of the then-surviving authors (Cecil Schwalbe and Terry Johnson) knows the origin of that maximum length and both told me that they have never seen a Mohave rattlesnake that large. While the source of the maximum length listed in Lowe, Schwalbe and Johnson (1986) remains elusive, I have noticed that it could be the result of transposing two digits of Klauber's (1972) published record. I have listed measurements in this book in English units but Klauber's data was recorded in metric units, including the maximum length for Mohave rattlesnakes as 1,231 millimeters (mm) and he was (and continues to be) likely the most quoted source for such measurements. If we transpose the two middle digits of Klauber's measurement and convert it to feet by the most likely method (1,321 mm/25.4 = 52.0 inches/12), we get the maximum measurement used in Lowe et al. (1986): 4.3 feet.

Ernst and Ernst (2003) listed the maximum total body length for Mohave rattlesnakes as "140 cm" (55.1 inches) without identifying a source for the measurement. Nine years later, however, they (Ernst and Ernst, 2012) listed the maximum total body length as 137.3 cm (54.1 inches), citing Tennant (1984). Degenhardt, Painter and Price (1996) also published 140 cm (55.1 inches) as the maximum length without providing a source and recent communication with the surviving authors has not yielded a basis for that record. There is a long history of accounts in field guides and handbooks, going back at least to 1957 (Wright and Wright), listing the maximum length in the 50–51 inch range. However, I can find no references in these publications supporting this measurement, including in the 17 references given for the Mohave rattlesnake by Wright and Wright (1957, 1962).

Then on 16 September 2014, James Hicks (Bangor University, UK) and Mrinalini (University of Rochester, NY) captured a male Mohave rattlesnake in Eloy, Pinal County, Arizona, that measured 1,236 mm (48.7 inches) total length (Mrinalini et al., 2015). The live snake was measured several times by carefully straightening it by hand against a metal rule with its anterior body in a clear plastic restraint tube and marking the length when the snake voluntarily straightened the portion of its body inside the tube. Thus, the collectors are quite confident in the measurement. As of this writing, the snake is in the live collection of the Chiricahua Desert Museum in Rodeo, New Mexico.

Thus, the maximum body lengths (including the tail without the rattle) I have been able to authenticate for the Mohave rattlesnake are 48.7 in. (1,236 mm) for males and 36.3 in. (923 mm) for females. Males typically have longer tails compared to their body length than females. Using Klauber's data sheets that contain these measurements (169 males and 307 females), average tail length as a percentage of total body length was 7.4% (range 4.1–10.5%) for males and 5.5% (range 3.4–7.4%) for females.

Body Mass

Mass (weight) is much more variable than length, due to the fact that snakes eat large infrequent meals that are often enormous compared to their body mass. Such meals can weigh nearly as much as the rattlesnake, meaning that the snake can nearly double its body weight in the time it takes to swallow a big meal – usually less than an hour. Of course, body mass returns to "normal" as the meal is digested and the resulting feces are voided. And pregnant females weigh much more than when they are not pregnant and then drop 30–50% of that weight during birth.

Note on the next page how mass variability increases with length, due primarily to how recently each snake had fed and the reproductive status of females. But you can see that body mass ranges roughly from less than an ounce for newborns that are 10–12 inches long, to almost a pound at three feet. Keep that in mind the next time you hear a claim about a giant rattlesnake weighing many pounds (see Chapter 12).

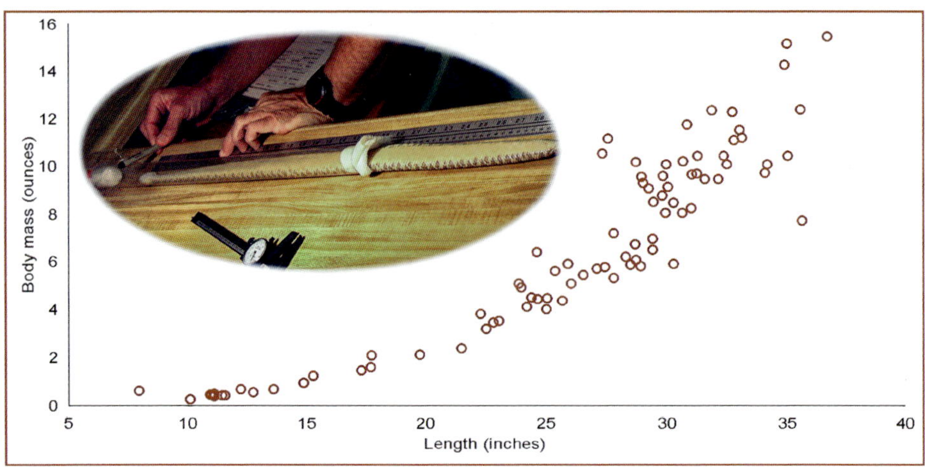

Laurence Klauber recorded body mass on few of his data sheets, probably because many of the specimens had been preserved for a long time when he examined them. However, I have charted total length (body plus tail without the rattle) and body mass here, using the 85 live animals processed during my 40-month field study in California.

Pattern and Coloration

Mohave rattlesnakes are prominently marked with a series of dark dorsal "diamonds" narrowly bordered by darker scales surrounded by a row of lighter scales, with the diamonds transitioning into transverse body bands near the tail.

The dorsal diamonds often just touch at the midline, especially on the front half of the snake, but they are sometimes separated by one or two scale rows of background color. Lateral spots are usually present on the sides and are the same color as the center of the dorsal diamonds, although smaller and less distinct than the dorsal markings. These lateral spots coincide, but are not always aligned, with the diamonds. The background color is lighter than the center of the diamonds and the last couple of scale rows adjacent to the ventral scales, with the exception of the lateral spots, are often lighter still. In the transition from diamonds to bands near the tail, the diamonds become separated and they gradually lose their contrasting dark and light borders. Near the tail, the transverse bands are uniformly colored like the center of anterior diamonds and merge with the lateral spots, usually making them wider near the midline than on the sides. There is little or no speckling in the dorsal pattern, making the pattern edges generally well defined.

The overall color of Mohave rattlesnakes is quite variable but is usually dominated by a greenish hue. Some animals can be pale green while others are considerably darker. This green hue can vary with temperature (cool snake = darker, warm snake = lighter) and the shedding (ecdysis) cycle, with freshly shed animals being more colorful. But in some Mohaves, the greenish hue is virtually absent, leaving the snake colored in shades of tan, light brown and/or gray. The belly is generally unmarked with a pale greenish or yellowish tint.

Throughout most of the Mohave rattlesnake's range, the tail is ringed with alternating black (or dark gray) and grayish-white rings, with the dark rings noticeably narrower than the light rings. These dark tail rings are often irregularly spaced and sometimes fragmented or at least offset at the dorsal centerline. Dark tail rings at the base of the tail tend to blend with the background body color. In northern Mohave County, Arizona, near the western end of the Grand Canyon, the pale tail rings tend to be replaced by the background body color and the darker tail rings are wider and brownish in color. Thus, in this population, the characteristic tail ring colors are sometimes replaced by a continuation of the body colors near the tail. One of the most consistent pattern characters of Mohave rattlesnakes, which can often be spotted in photographs, is the angle of the light postocular stripe, as it sweeps down and rearward from just behind the eye. In Mohaves, this stripe rapidly bends rearward, passing above the corner of the mouth.

Another small but useful trait is found on the other end of the snake: the live rattle segment. The newest rattle segment is attached to the tail and full of live tissue, unlike all of the older hollow segments. In most Mohaves, this live segment is usually two-toned: partly black and partly a pale yellow or cream color, although the black is occasionally missing entirely.

Odd (and Rare) Colors and Patterns

As with all animals, individuals are occasionally born with genetic mutations that dramatically alter their appearance. Many of these mutations are so harmful that the creature is doomed to a very early death, as with the baby two-headed Mohave rattlesnake pictured in the predecessor to Field and Stream Magazine in 1909 (Kelly, 1909; Cardwell, 2016).

Less lethal mutations often affect color and pattern. I know of one leucistic (i.e., skin pigmentation almost entirely absent but with normally-colored eyes) female Mohave rattlesnake from Kern County, California (Cardwell and Alexander, 2006) but none verified from other areas. Photos of an identical-looking animal were posted to iNaturalist on 2 October 2017 (observation no. 8221807). As you will read on the webpage, it seems likely that this animal is a captive-born offspring of the wild-caught Kern County female described in Cardwell and Alexander (2006).

This pale yellowish Mohave rattlesnake was photographed crossing a road near Lancaster in Los Angeles County, California. Interestingly, the pattern disappears near the tail, leaving no obvious tail rings. The postocular facial stripes are also absent. Photo courtesy Chris DeGroof.

A one-of-a-kind patternless Mohave rattlesnake captured in northwestern Maricopa County, Arizona. At the time of this writing, it is in the live collection at the Chiricahua Desert Museum in Rodeo, New Mexico.

A leucistic female Mohave rattlesnake from Kern County, California.

A small female Mohave rattlesnake with an unusual striped neck, being courted by a normally-patterned male. San Bernardino County, California.

This pale Mohave rattlesnake was photographed near Nuevo Casa Grandes in Chihuahua, Mexico. Photo courtesy of Daniel Montoya Ferrer.

This very dark Mohave rattlesnake was encountered near Lancaster in Los Angeles County, California. Photo courtesy of Kimball Garrett.

These three young Mohave rattlesnakes are all from Mexico. They were photographed in (top-bottom) the states of (A) Coahuila, (B) Nuevo Leon and (C) Zacatecas and they illustrate the color variation found in the species. Photos courtesy of Michael Price.

A Mohave rattlesnake with an unusually indistinct dorsal pattern from Pima County, Arizona.

The blunt stub of the "rattleless" Mohave rattlesnake from Adelanto, California. It cannot be confused with the tapered pointed tails of other kinds of snakes.

Due to irregular dorsal markings that are common on the neck of otherwise normally colored and patterned Mohave rattlesnakes, some limited striping on the neck is not too uncommon.

Physical deformities are usually due to injury rather than birth defect. Whether genetic or traumatic in origin, weird individuals are so rare that I used to not mention them during my rattlesnake presentations. Then one day years ago, I told an auditorium full of people that every rattlesnake has at least one rattle segment – even the "rattleless" rattlesnake (*Crotalus catalinensis*) of Isla Santa Catalina near La Paz, Mexico. But a guy in the audience stuck his hand in the air and claimed to have a rattleless carcass in his freezer. I made arrangements to see it and sure enough, he did! It turned out to be an adult male Mohave rattlesnake with a blunt stub for a tail. Close examination, x-rays, and consultation with a veterinarian revealed that part of the tail was also missing – almost certainly a healed injury from long ago. The carcass was deposited in the herpetology collection of the Los Angeles County Museum of Natural History (specimen no. LACM159667; see Cardwell and Banashek, 2006).

Scale Counts and Arrangements

In his description of *Crotalus scutulatus scutulatus*, Gloyd (1940:200) listed scale counts as follows: minimum scales between supraoculars usually two, mid-body scale rows usually 25, ventrals 166-190 (average 178) in males and 167-192 (average181) in females, subcaudals 21-29 (average 25) in males and 15-25 (average 19) in females; supralabials 12-18 (average 15) and infralabials 12-18 (average 16). Corresponding averages I have calculated from Klauber's data sheets are identical.

Probably the best generalization that can be made regarding the size and arrangement of the crown scales (on top of the head) of Mohave rattlesnakes is that they are enlarged and highly irregular. Most references list two crown scales between the supraoculars as being diagnostic for identifying Mohave rattlesnakes. However, Klauber (1930:118) commented long ago that too much emphasis is often placed on two scales bridging the supraoculars when trying to identify Mohaves, yet that cautionary note is frequently overlooked by recent authors. Combining Klauber's 473 Mohave rattlesnake data sheets that contain crown scale data with my own series of 85 animals from my 2001–2005 study, the supraoculars were separated by two scales in 86% of animals, by three scales in 12%, and by four scales in 2%.

Thus, while the supraoculars are separated by two scales in the great majority of Mohave rattlesnakes, they are separated by three or four scales in almost 15% of Mohaves – contrary to many published keys and other references. I have never examined a specimen with more than four scales separating the supraoculars. And although Klauber's data sheets indicated one animal with five scales (specimen SDSNH 4598), I counted only four.

Another unique characteristic of almost all Mohave rattlesnakes is a large crescent-shaped scale bordering the rear of each supraocular. These crescentic scales are often notched, sometimes deeply, opposite the supraocular. On a small proportion of individuals, this notch actually divides the scale in half, giving the appearance that the crescentic scale is missing but this can be recognized with some practice. As with many paired scale configurations, I

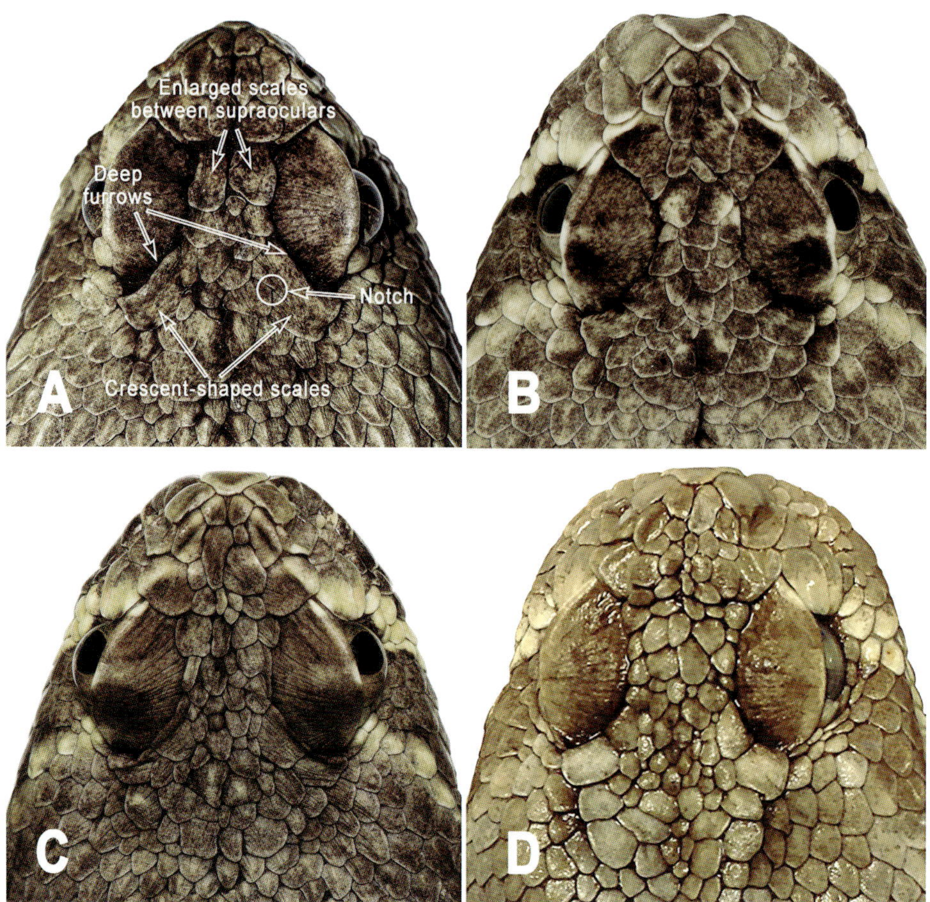

Examples of crown scales of Mohave rattlesnakes: (A) the characteristic two scales separating the supraoculars, as well as the crescent-shaped scales behind the supraoculars – one entire and one notched; (B) an animal with a three-scale "bridge" between supraoculars; (C) a four-scale bridge; and (D) Klauber's specimen no. SDSNH4598. Note the divided crescent-shaped scales in B, C and D.

have seen Mohaves with one crescentic crown scale divided while the opposite one is intact. Finally, the point where the supraoculars tuck under the crescent-shaped scales on the heads of Mohave rattlesnakes is usually marked by a particularly deep and dark furrow.

DISTRIBUTION

Mohave rattlesnakes occur naturally across a broad swath of arid habitats extending from the western end of the Mohave Desert in California's Los Angeles and Kern Counties, eastward and southeastward across the southwestern half of Arizona and throughout the Mexican Plateau, deep into mainland Mexico. The edges of this distribution extend into southern Nevada (as far north as Lincoln County), the extreme southwestern edge of Utah, southwestern New

Mexico, and the Big Bend region of Texas. Its range comes very close to the northern end of the Sea of Cortez but they are apparently absent from Baja California. This distribution encompasses much of the Mohave, Sonoran, and Chihuahuan Deserts, as well as the Mexican Plateau.

California

The distribution of Mohave rattlesnakes in California's desert reaches as far west as the foothills of the San Gabriel, San Bernardino and Tehachapi Mountains and north to the southern margin of Inyo County. Farther east in California, it has always been perplexing to me that Mohave rattlesnakes seem to disappear south of Interstate 40 and east of the Marine Corps' 29 Palms Air Ground Combat Center. I know of no museum specimens from this area and only one photograph of a Mohave purportedly from there (iNaturalist observation no. 3309079), despite the creosote bush scrub habitat being virtually identical and uninterrupted from farther north and west.

I know of no reliable records of Mohave rattlesnakes south of San Bernardino County in eastern California; so there seem to be none in Riverside or Imperial Counties – although there are Mohaves on the other side of the Colorado River in Arizona's La Paz and Yuma Counties. A single photo posted on iNaturalist in the spring of 2018 clearly shows a Mohave rattlesnake in the debris from a fallen Joshua Tree and gives coordinates in the middle of Joshua Tree National Park about 12 miles inside Riverside County. There are, however, no Joshua Trees anywhere close to the location provided. There are three museum specimens at the Los Angeles County Natural History Museum that were recorded from the northwestern edge of Joshua Tree National Park within San Bernardino County. According to long-time JTNP herpetologist Harold De Lisle (2017), Mohave rattlesnakes have been found "only along the northern edge of the park" but may now have been wiped out within the park.

Arizona

A series of northwest-to-southeast mountain ranges, known collectively as the Mogollon Rim, divides Arizona into desert to the southwest and the Colorado Plateau to the northeast. Mohave rattlesnakes are absent from the mountains of the Mogollon Rim and from the Colorado Plateau. They are, however, abundant in the Sonoran Desert southwest of the Mogollon Rim, in Mohave Desert habitat to the northwest and in Chihuahuan Desert habitat to the southeast, as well as in semi-desert grassland and conifer woodland habitats in Santa Cruz and Cochise Counties. They are also found in isolated areas of similar habitat in the counties of Mohave, Yavapai, Gila, and Greenlee. Such areas include grassland and conifer woodland areas in places like the Chino and Verde Valleys in Yavapai County and around Roosevelt Reservoir and Globe in Gila County.

Nevada

Mohave rattlesnakes in Nevada are primarily limited to Clark County, the adjacent southern corner of Nye County, and extending up to the area around Mesquite.

Utah

Mohaves are only found in Utah in the extreme southwestern corner of Washington County, just across the boundaries from Nevada and Arizona.

New Mexico

The only place in New Mexico where Mohave rattlesnakes are consistently encountered is in Hidalgo County, south of Interstate 10 and west of the town of Animas. And since there are recent records of Mohaves in El Paso County, Texas, it would not be surprising to encounter an occasional Mohave rattlesnake in New Mexico's adjacent Dona Ana County.

Texas

Mohaves are common in the Big Bend area of Texas all the way from Brewster Country up to El Paso County and as far east as Fort Stockton, well over a hundred miles from the Rio Grande.

Mexico

Although outside the scope of this book, Mohave rattlesnakes are also found in Sonora and south through Chihuahua and the Mexican Plateau as far as the states of Mexico, Puebla, and Veracruz (Klauber, 1972; Campbell and Lamar, 2004).

Western diamondback rattlesnakes (*Crotalus atrox*), like this Pima County, Arizona, animal, are the most common rattlesnakes throughout most of the arid southwestern United States and are often confused with Mohave rattlesnakes.

3 Identification: Is This Rattlesnake a Mohave?

HOW DO YOU TELL A MOHAVE RATTLESNAKE FROM OTHER RATTLESNAKES?

There is no single observable trait that allows us to reliably identify every Mohave rattlesnake. All of the traits are somewhat variable and the most credible identifications are based on evaluation of multiple traits.

A word of caution here: Be sure to read Chapter 13: Avoiding rattlesnake bites. Some of the best identifying characteristics for Mohave rattlesnakes are too small to see from a safe distance – and I like to tell people to stay at least twice the length of the snake away from any rattlesnake. Good photographs, including views of the top of the head and the tail, that are in sharp focus and taken from a safe distance will usually permit a reliable identification. But there is little reason to get too close to a live rattlesnake to determine its species. And never handle a dead rattlesnake or a severed head. Even if someone has already been bitten, confirming the species is not critical for treatment, since the same antivenoms are used for all North American rattlesnakes. Trying to identify the rattlesnake only risks someone else being bitten and wastes time that should be used to get the victim to a hospital and antivenom. It doesn't hurt to take a quick overall photo of the snake from a safe distance, then leave the snake alone and head for the nearest hospital without delay. See Chapter 14 for more complete first aid recommendations.

To recognize Mohave rattlesnakes, first familiarize yourself with Chapter 2 – their description and where they are found. Do not fall into the common trap that any greenish-colored rattlesnake must be a Mohave or any rattlesnake bite that produces neurotoxic symptoms must have been from a Mohave rattlesnake. Some Mohaves are not green, several other rattlesnakes produce neurotoxins, and there are not likely to be undiscovered populations of Mohaves far outside of their known distribution. In the following pages, I will focus on how to tell a Mohave rattlesnake apart from other rattlesnakes within their range.

Throughout much of their distribution, Mohave rattlesnakes are desert animals and are common in the same places as western diamondbacks (*Crotalus atrox*) and sidewinders (*Crotalus cerastes*). While sidewinders are very distinctive and easily identified by their supraocular "horns" and lack of dorsal diamond markings, differentiating Mohaves from western diamondbacks can be a challenge (Bush and Cardwell, 1999).

The supraocular "horns" protruding above the eyes make the little sidewinder (*Crotalus cerastes*) easy to identify. Adults are no more than two feet long. This one is from Pima County, Arizona.

In grassland habitats and in juniper-covered foothills, Mohaves can be confused with western rattlesnakes (*Crotalus oreganus*), black-tailed rattlesnakes (*Crotalus molossus* and *C. ornatus*), prairie rattlesnakes (*Crotalus viridis*), and massasaugas (*Sistrurus tergeminus*). And, although they inhabit foothill and mountain habitats not occupied by Mohave rattlesnakes, some Arizona black rattlesnakes (*Crotalus cerberus*) can look surprisingly like Mohaves found not far away.

It may help to understand that Mohave rattlesnakes are only distantly related to western diamondbacks while they are closely related to western and prairie rattlesnakes. Therefore, Mohaves share some traits with western and prairie rattlesnakes that they do not share with western diamondbacks, as will be explained below.

MOHAVE RATTLESNAKES vs. WESTERN DIAMONDBACKS

In the United States, these two species are found together throughout the arid areas of southern and western Arizona, extreme southwestern New Mexico, and extreme western Texas – mostly in the Big Bend area. Their ranges come very close to one another, if not slightly overlapping, in southeastern San Bernardino County in California and southern Clark County in Nevada. Generally speaking, both are relatively large rattlesnakes (although the western diamondback gets bigger) with diamond-shaped dorsal markings and a more or less black and white-ringed tail.

Most (but not all) Mohave rattlesnakes are greenish in overall color but some can be primarily brown and/or grayish. Western diamondbacks are various shades of brown, gray, and/or sometimes reddish brown but not green. So a significantly greenish overall color is likely a Mohave but lack of a greenish hue does not exclude a Mohave.

The dorsal diamonds are bordered with white scales and the dorsal pattern is almost always heavily speckled in the western diamondback, while the Mohave's dorsal diamonds are rarely, if ever, bordered with white and their dorsal pattern is rather crisp and well defined with little or no speckling. The alternating tail rings in western diamondbacks are almost always very black and very white and the black and white rings are usually similar in width. In Mohave rattlesnakes, the dark tail rings are usually narrower than the light rings – but not always. Additionally, the color of the tail rings is more variable in Mohave rattlesnakes. The light rings are sometimes light gray or even light tan and the dark rings can be dark gray or even the same greenish-brown or tan color as the adjacent body. But the tail rings are occasionally stark black and white like western diamondbacks.

Some Mohave rattlesnakes, like this female from Pima County, Arizona, lack the characteristic green tint, adding to the confusion with western diamondbacks.

The tail rings on western diamondbacks (left) are almost always high contrast – very black and very white, but the black and white rings are not always the same width, as is often suggested. Tail rings on most Mohave rattlesnakes (right) are usually much more subdued, often just dark and light shades of gray, and the dark rings are usually (but not always) narrower than the light ones in Mohaves. Also note the speckling on the body scales of the diamondback, which is missing on the Mohave.

Also on the tail, the new live rattle segment of western diamondbacks is usually completely black while, in Mohaves, it is partly or entirely cream-colored.

Both Mohave rattlesnakes and western diamondbacks have two light facial stripes on each side of the face, one just in front of the eye and the other just behind (called preocular and postocular stripes, respectively) and the postocular stripe is important for distinguishing Mohaves from western diamondbacks. In diamondbacks, the postocular stripe drops down to intersect with the mouth and it is usually parallel to the preocular stripe. In Mohave

Compare facial stripes on the western diamondback (left) and the Mohave rattlesnake (right).

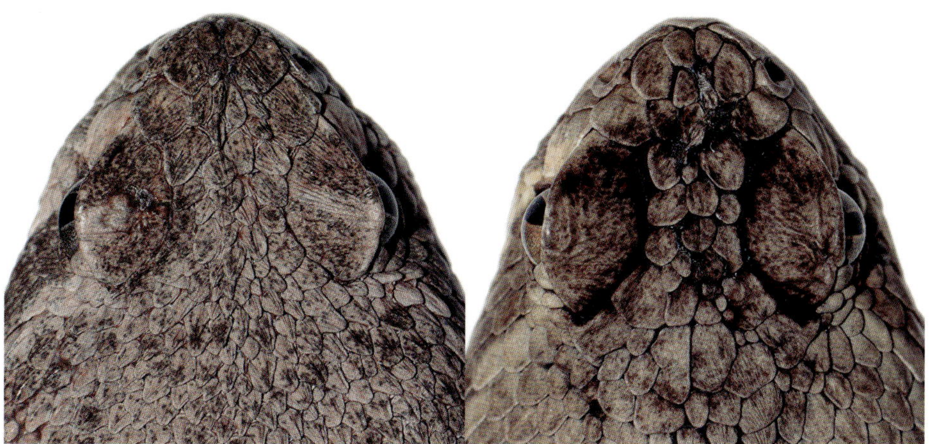

Crown scales on a western diamondback (left) compared to a Mohave rattlesnake (right). Most Mohaves have two scales separating the supraocular scales but three (like this one) or four are not uncommon. And while most western diamondbacks have much smaller scales between the supraoculars, some have as few as three or four (like the one above). A consistent difference is the jumble of enlarged scales that spill out behind the supraoculars on Mohaves but seem to be missing on western diamondbacks.

rattlesnakes, the postocular stripe bends rearward towards the neck and does not intersect with the mouth.

The characteristics described above can be viewed from a safe distance and are even useful to identify rattlesnakes in photographs. But the following characters are too small to be examined from a safe distance on a live rattlesnake.

In western diamondbacks, the area on top of the head, including between and around the supraoculars, is covered with small scales of mostly uniform size. But in Mohaves, these crown scales are enlarged and the arrangement is highly variable. The supraoculars in most Mohave rattlesnakes are separated by two large scales but a few Mohaves have three or four scales between the supraoculars, while four scales seem to be the minimum in diamondbacks.

Diamondbacks also lack the pair of distinctive crescent-shaped scales just behind the supraoculars and they lack the deep furrows, where the edges of the supraoculars tuck under the crown scales on Mohaves.

Prairie rattlesnake (*Crotalus viridis*). Most other rattlesnakes, including Mohaves, typically have only two internasal scales in contact with the top of the rostral.

MOHAVE RATTLESNAKES vs. WESTERN AND PRAIRIE RATTLESNAKES

Western rattlesnakes (*Crotalus oreganus*) and prairie rattlesnakes (*C. viridis*) are more closely related to one another than to Mohaves and can be differentiated from Mohave rattlesnakes by the same method. Tail rings are usually present on most western and prairie rattlesnakes but they are greatly subdued compared to Mohaves and diamondbacks. The tail rings are the same colors as the body markings on westerns and prairies and the light rings are quite narrow compared to the dark rings. The tail rings on these snakes are not black and white – not even close. Maybe the most reliable single trait to identify western and prairie rattlesnakes is the smallest and hardest to see safely: the number of internasal scales touching the rostral scale. In other rattlesnakes, including Mohaves, only two internasals come into contact with the top of the rostral. But in westerns and prairies, four internasals usually touch the rostral. Both western and prairie rattlesnakes also have many small crown scales between the supraoculars, unlike Mohaves.

Prairie rattlesnakes overlap with Mohave rattlesnake distribution in southwestern New Mexico and western Texas. Their coloration is often rather greenish but their dorsal markings are more oval than diamond-shaped, the edges are well-defined and there is usually considerable space between them.

Western rattlesnakes overlap slightly with Mohaves in California, along the desert/foothill ecotone at the base of the San Gabriel and San Bernardino Mountains in Los Angeles and San Bernardino Counties and along the base of the Tehachapi and southern Sierra Nevada Mountains in Kern County and probably the southern edge of Inyo County. The dorsal markings of western rattlesnakes are similar to those of Mohaves: more or less diamond-shaped and touching or slightly overlapping at the center. Their coloration is usually shades of gray, brown and black; with only occasionally a slight greenish tint. Facial stripes are similar to Mohave rattlesnakes and therefore useless to tell these species apart. But the tail rings and head scales, along with the dorsal pattern of prairies, will almost always yield a confident identification.

MOHAVE RATTLESNAKES vs. BLACK-TAILED RATTLESNAKES

Black-tailed rattlesnakes (*Crotalus molossus* and *C. ornatus*) can be quickly distinguished from Mohave rattlesnakes by their obvious sooty black tails, including the base rattle segment. In some individuals, the tail may be very dark gray or slightly brownish and some very faint tail rings are occasionally visible. But on first glance, the tail will look entirely black, or nearly so, and that excludes Mohave rattlesnakes.

Western black-tailed rattlesnake (*Crotalus molossus*). Although this rattlesnake has some enlarged scales between the supraoculars, it is easily distinguished from a Mohave rattlesnake. The sooty black tail is distinctive, although some faint lighter rings are visible on some individuals. The dark area in front of the eyes and the lack of a postocular light stripe are also noteworthy.

Additionally, the dark dorsal markings are jagged and irregular and extend down both sides of the snake to form narrow bands. The background color between these markings can be tan, gray, yellow or even golden – making some of them quite beautiful. The top of the head usually has some large plates in front of the supraoculars and sometimes between them, but this area is characteristically uniform black or dark brown in blacktails but not in Mohaves. The crescent-shaped scales found on the crown of Mohaves are missing in black-tailed rattlesnakes. A broad dark stripe drops at an angle from the eye in blacktails but it lacks the light pre- and postocular stripes of Mohaves.

MOHAVE RATTLESNAKES vs. MASSASAUGAS

Massasaugas (*Sistrurus tergeminus*) are small rattlesnakes that are seldom encountered. They overlap with the Mohave rattlesnake's range only in tiny corners of three states: southeastern Arizona, southwestern New Mexico, and western Texas. Massasaugas belong to the other rattlesnake genus *Sistrurus*, characterized by the entire top of the head being covered in a well-organized pattern of nine large symmetrically-arranged plates – a characteristic they share with most of our harmless snakes, as well as venomous cottonmouths, copperheads and coralsnakes. On first glance, massasaugas look like small prairie rattlesnakes, with large adults being only about two feet in length. Dark dorsal markings are oval or irregularly-shaped (not diamonds) and well-separated from one another. If tail rings are present, they are blended into the adjacent body markings and of the same shades of gray and brown. Massasaugas are not easily confused with Mohave rattlesnakes.

Western massasauga (*Sistrurus tergeminus*)

Arizona black rattlesnakes (*Crotalus cerberus*) like this one typically lose most of their more distinct juvenile markings as they mature. In any event, they can be easily identified from a safe distance by their predominantly gray or black coloration, indistinct tail rings, and mountainous habitat. This one was encountered in Pima County, Arizona.

MOHAVE RATTLESNAKES vs. ARIZONA BLACK RATTLESNAKES

Arizona black rattlesnakes (*Crotalus cerberus*) are closely related to western and prairie rattlesnakes. Especially as juveniles and young adults, Arizona black rattlesnakes can be difficult to discern from these relatives, being particularly similar to western rattlesnakes. As their common name suggests, many adult Arizona black rattlesnakes are almost entirely black; so much so, in fact, that their dorsal markings may be completely hidden. Nonetheless, the shift from lighter-colored and distinctly-patterned juveniles to adult coloration is highly variable. Although many become black, some others retain their light-colored patterns as adults while other adults are intermediate. Lighter-colored adults may be many shades including browns, grays, and olive.While the mountainous locations where Arizona black rattlesnakes are found should preclude them from being mistaken for Mohaves, a few can look remarkably like Mohave rattlesnakes at first glance (e.g., Campbell and Lamar, 2004: plates 903 & 904). Nonetheless, they can be distinguished from Mohave rattlesnakes by the same criteria suggested for western and prairie rattlesnakes previously. In fact, details of the facial scales are even more unique in Arizona black rattlesnakes. For example, more than four internasals often border the rostral scale. For additional details, see Davis et al. (2016).

This large male Mohave rattlesnake from Pima County, Arizona, is investigating the photographer by sampling chemical clues in the air with its moist tongue. Note the predominantly unspeckled pattern, without darker scales sprinkled on the sides of the animal, as well as no fine speckling within individual scales, especially on the face. Compare to photos of western diamondbacks on previous pages..

The First Mohave Rattlesnake

HOW LONG HAVE MOHAVE RATTLESNAKES BEEN AROUND?

The science of "phylogeny" is the study of the evolutionary development of a group of organisms and the relationship between the various members. Much of phylogeny boils down to figuring out how long ago two species alive today shared a common ancestor.

Most of this is done by comparing organisms genetically: the DNA of closely related species will have fewer mismatches than the DNA of more distant relatives. But we are not talking about uncles and cousins here. While the concept is similar, the time frame is not. Rather than decades or even centuries, phylogenetic analyses usually deal in millions of years!

How in the world can scientists do that? Well, a complete explanation is far beyond the scope of this book – as well as my ability to explain it. But I can give you the basics. All DNA is made up of long chains of only four "nucleotides," which are the biochemical building blocks of DNA, and we know that there are certain rules about how they can be arranged. Mutations to DNA happen all the time, usually due to mistakes as DNA is copied during cell division, as well as external causes like exposure to ionizing radiation. These mistakes can take several forms such as a nucleotide being entirely missing, being replaced by one of the other three nucleotides, or being damaged so that the molecule no longer functions as a nucleotide.

Biologists who specialize in "phylogenetics" have estimated how long it takes for a certain number of changes (mutations) to accumulate in an organism's "genome" (the entire set of genes in an organism). Then, by comparing the number of differences between the genomes of different organisms, the time it has taken for those changes to accumulate can be estimated – telling us about how long ago they were the same organism (the common ancestor). These genetic "clocks" are not exact for a variety of reasons; maybe the most obvious being that natural selection is a very slow process and new species do not just appear one day. Rather, existing forms slowly adapt as their environment gradually changes around them. So make no mistake, this is good science – especially as many different scientists around the world, working on different groups of organisms and using different techniques, come up with similar results.

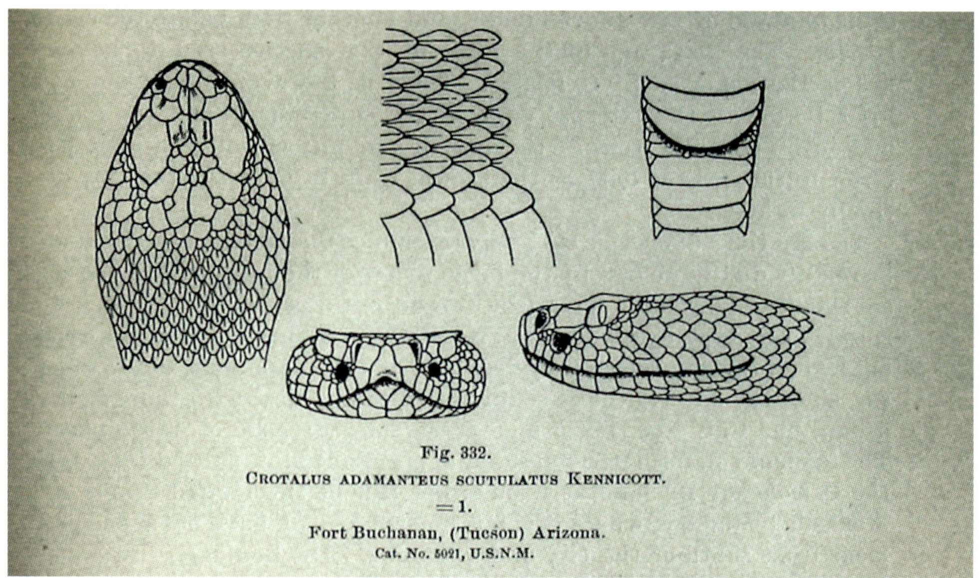

This drawing, published in 1900, was made from one of the first specimens of the Mohave rattlesnake received at the Smithsonian Institution in 1860. The drawing was published by Edward Cope in his mistaken identification of the type specimen of *Crotalus scutulatus*.

It is also interesting and useful to point out that much of what we know about genetics and gene mutations has been learned from fruit flies! Why fruit flies? Because they are easy to culture in a lab, nobody cares about them (scientists can do all sorts of terrible things to them – like radiation exposure – that would never be allowed on "higher" animals like mice) and you have results in twelve days (the time it takes for adult fruit flies to produce adult offspring, compared to weeks, months or years for "higher" animals). There are also ways of validating genetic clocks, such as ageing the rock surrounding any available fossils using radioisotope analysis, which is very precise.

Using such techniques, one of the most widely accepted analyses of rattlesnake phylogeny is the study published by Jacobo Reyes-Velasco and his colleagues in 2013. Theirs and multiple previous studies have concluded that the closest living relatives of Mohave rattlesnakes are the prairie and western rattlesnakes. In their work, Reyes-Velasco and his colleagues calculated the time that Mohave rattlesnakes and the ancestor of prairie and western rattlesnakes diverged from a common ancestor to be between about 4.4 and 1.8 MYA (million years ago; Reyes-Velasco et al., 2013). A more recent study led by Drew Schield (Schield et al., 2018) studied the relationship between present-day Mohave rattlesnake populations throughout the species' distribution.

Through genetic analysis of extensive new sampling, they identified four distinct lineages and the approximate times they became separated – that is, when gene flow between them was interrupted.

Schield and his colleagues found genetic evidence that the original ancestral Mohave rattlesnake population was divided into northern and southern groups around 3.4 MYA, probably very shortly after they split from the ancestral prairie rattlesnakes. The location of this genetic intergrade zone corresponds to the rise in elevation of about 3,000 feet from the Chihuahuan Desert to the Central Mexican Plateau.

Later, each of these groups was divided further. At about 2.1 MYA, the southern-most population became isolated and evolved into that we now call a subspecies of the Mohave rattlesnake, known as the Huamantlan rattlesnake (*Crotalus scutulatus salvini*). Then, about 1.5 MYA, the northern group became separated at the continental divide in an area spanning the southeast corner of Arizona, the southwest corner New Mexico, and adjacent Sonora and Chihuahua – a region known as the "Cochise Filter." This resulted in Mohave rattlesnakes in the Mojave and Sonoran Deserts now being subtly different (genetically) from those in the Chihuahuan Desert. Similar studies of many other desert organisms have shown the high elevation in the Cochise Filter to have been an important influence during the climatic cycles of the Pliocene and early Pleistocene Epochs, with populations east and west of the filter being isolated and evolving separately during cold times, then reconnecting and interbreeding again during warmer periods. (See map and chart, next page) So there is no doubt that Mohave rattlesnakes have been crawling around for a very long time. But when did people first notice them?

SEARCH FOR THE "TYPE SPECIMEN"

One of the most prevalent myths about Mohave rattlesnakes involves their origin. Many folks insist that Mohaves are not ordinary rattlesnakes. Rather, they claim Mohaves are the product of some recent and mysterious process or event. Proponents of the recent origin rumors have sometimes pointed out that there is no "type specimen" for *Crotalus scutulatus*, as exists for most other organisms. That argument was difficult to refute – until recently.

Laurence M. Klauber (1883–1968) was a brilliant mathematician and inventor with an engineering degree from Stanford University who rose through the ranks to become president (1946) and CEO (1949) of San Diego Gas and Electric Company. While he was passionate about many things, one of his main interests was rattlesnakes. He spent much of his spare time studying rattlesnakes – lots of them, amassing a personal collection of more than 8,600

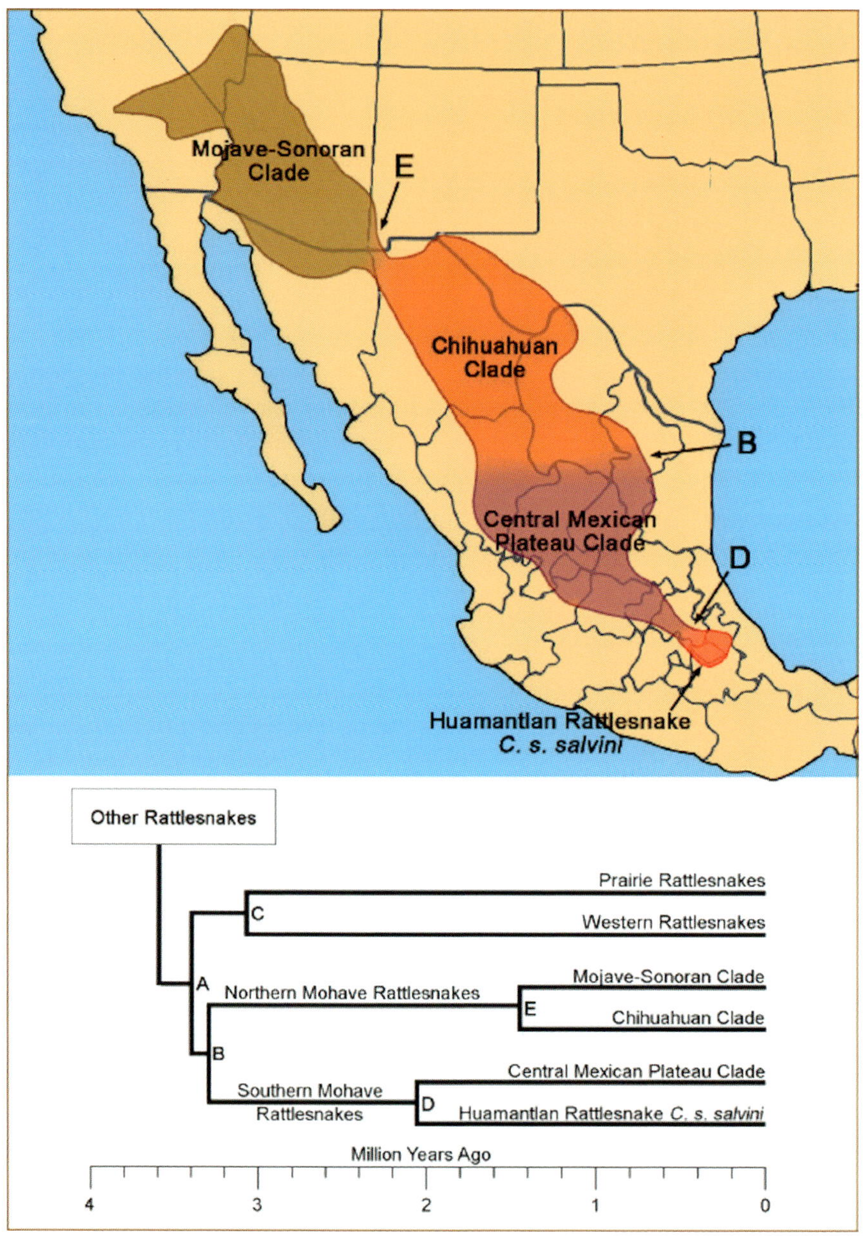

Map adapted from Schield et al., 2018; phylogenetic tree (bottom) adapted from Reyes-Velasco et al., 2013.

preserved specimens that he eventually donated to the San Diego Natural History Museum. He also examined many other specimens preserved in public and private museums and universities around the country.

Klauber's encyclopedic knowledge of rattlesnakes culminated in *Rattlesnakes – Their Habits, Life Histories, and Influence on Mankind*, a two-volume, 1,400 page book, summarizing what was known about rattlesnakes when it was first printed by the University of California Press in 1956. An updated edition was published in 1972, prepared by Klauber shortly before he succumbed to heart disease. His analytical style and attention to detail has made Klauber's *Rattlesnakes* the primary scholarly reference upon which biologists have based subsequent rattlesnake research. In a footnote to the species account for the Mohave rattlesnake on page 42 of the first (1956) edition of *Rattlesnakes* (and on page 47 of the 1972 edition), Klauber wrote:

> "Cope (1900, p. 1160) refers to USNM 5021 as the type of *C. scutulatus*, but there is nothing in the museum catalogue to confirm this. USNM 5021 is actually the head of a *C. v. cerberus* or *C. v. helleri*. USNM 5027 is a *scutulatus*, and may have been the specimen Cope had in mind. Both specimens were sent in by Dr. B. J. D. Irwin, and, although ostensibly from Fort Buchanan, Arizona, may have come from California or elsewhere, as indicated by other specimens in the same shipment. USNM 5027 was originally catalogued as "*Caudisona lepturus*" under date of January 30, 1861. This may be a name originally contemplated by Kennicott for this species, which would suggest that this was the type, although Kennicott's counts of the labials are not the same as those of No. 5027."

Klauber was apparently the first to discover that the preserved snake in the Smithsonian Institution (aka United States National Museum or USNM), known as specimen number USNM 5021, could not be the original or "type" specimen of the Mohave rattlesnake, as had been reported by Edward Cope in 1900. He also noted that USNM 5027 was the correct species but did not match the details of the original description. In biological terms, a "type specimen" is the specific animal, permanently preserved in an institutional collection, from which a scientist first described a new species. For many years, the missing type specimen of the Mohave rattlesnake added apparent credibility to the idea that Mohaves have a very recent and unnatural origin.

Army Assistant Surgeon Bernard J. D. Irwin (left, circa 1863), collector of the type specimen of *Crotalus scutulatus*. Robert Kennicott (center, circa 1860s) originally described the species. Laurence M. Klauber (right, circa 1941) discovered Cope's error from 1900 and located the actual type specimen at the Philadelphia Academy of Natural Sciences in 1934. Photos: Courtesy John H. Fahey (Irwin), Smithsonian Institution Archives Image # SIA2011-1226 (Kennicott), and Archives of the Research Library, San Diego Natural History Museum (Klauber).

The original description of the Mohave rattlesnake was published in August 1861, the same year the Civil War began. The author, Robert Kennicott, was one of several young naturalists employed at the time by Spencer F. Baird, Assistant Secretary of the Smithsonian Institution, to catalog and describe new organisms being collected by military expeditions to the American West and shipped back to Washington, D.C. Although type specimens of new species described today must be carefully identified by museum and specimen number, it was not uncommon in 1861 to omit these details, which Kennicott did in this case. Kennicott was a member of both the Smithsonian Institution and the Academy of Natural Sciences of Philadelphia in those days and he published his description of "*Caudisona scutulata*" (now *Crotalus scutulatus*), as well as some others, in the Proceedings of the Academy of Natural Sciences of Philadelphia. Unfortunately, Kennicott died during an expedition to the Arctic in 1866 and was not available to consult with subsequent authors about his work.

Although the Mohave rattlesnake was mentioned by several variations of its Latin name in museum inventories and species checklists in the late 1800s, Cope was the first author to identify the type specimen in 1900. Writing in the Annual Report of the Board of Regents of the Smithsonian Institution published that year, he identified the type specimen as USNM 5021. This

Recent photos of the type specimen of *Crotalus scutulatus*, housed in the collection of the Academy of Natural Sciences of Philadelphia; specimen number ANSP 7069. Photos: Ned Gilmore, ANSP.

type specimen designation was unquestioned for half a century, until Klauber published *Rattlesnakes* (Klauber, 1956:42).

Fast forward to 1992. Collaboration between Ronald Heyer at the Smithsonian and John Cadle at the Academy of Natural Sciences of Philadelphia established that USNM 5027 had originally consisted of two specimens, one of which was transferred to Philadelphia long ago, becoming ANSP 7069. Cadle determined that the scale counts and other descriptive traits documented by Kennicott were consistent with ANSP 7069 and they concluded that ANSP 7069 is the animal originally described by Kennicott – the type specimen. Roy McDiarmid and his colleagues subsequently identified ANSP 7069 as the type specimen of *Crotalus scutulatus* in their 1999 book, *Snake Species of the World. A Taxonomic and Geographic Reference*, followed in 2004 by Jon Campbell and Bill Lamar in *The Venomous Reptiles of the Western Hemisphere*. Because I had such an interest in *Crotalus scutulatus* and in countering the many tall tales surrounding this animal, I began looking into the type specimen issue in 2008. My interest was piqued when I discovered in Cope's 1900 publication that he had provided detailed drawings, a fact not mentioned in the many references to this publication. Cope's drawings clearly showed the head scales of the snake he identified as the type, labeled USNM 5021.

I contacted Roy McDiarmid at the Smithsonian and he put me in contact with Steve Gotte and James Poindexter II. Wanting to examine USNM 5021 and 5027 myself, I originally asked for the specimens to be loaned to me (a courtesy frequently extended between institutions and biologists). When I

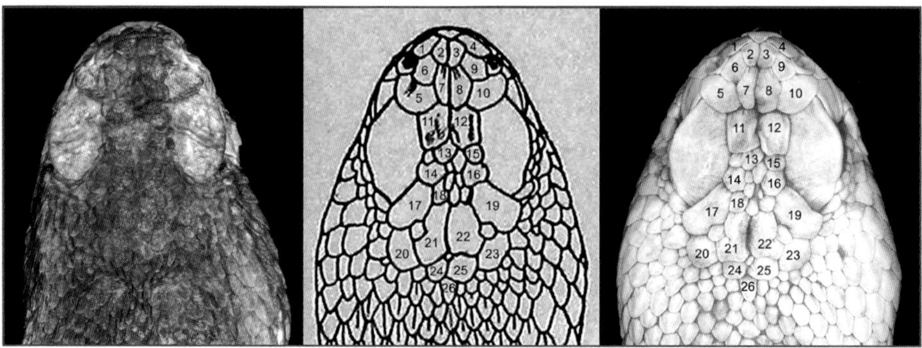

Comparison of specimens USNM 5021 (left), 5027 (right), and Cope's 1900 drawing (center) labeled as USNM 5021. Note similarity of numbered scales between Cope's drawing and USNM 5027. Photos: Steve Gotte and James Poindexter II, Smithsonian Institution; reprinted with permission from *Proceedings of the Biological Society of Washington* 126:11–16 (2013).

agreed that high-quality photographs would suffice, Steve and Jim provided me with exquisite photos of both snakes. Clearly, USNM 5021 was not a Mohave but USNM 5027 was. However, it was also obvious that Cope's 1900 drawing, identified as USNM 5021, was undoubtedly made from USNM 5027.

During this process, my Smithsonian colleagues found two very old specimen tags in the jar with USNM 5027. The older tag looked blank when first removed from the alcohol but Steve and Jim dried it, examined it under ultraviolet light, and discovered writing. After photographing the tag under UV light and digitally enhancing the contrast, "5027 *Crotalus Lepturus* Kenn" was visible on the first line and "Ft. Buchanan" and "Dr. Irwin" was visible on the second, with the possibility of something illegible between Ft. Buchanan and Dr. Irwin. Notably, the 2 and 7 in the specimen number were barely discernable, even after drying and enhanced UV photography. The more recent tag, however, was quite legible, bearing specimen number 5021, followed by "*Crotalus adamanteus scutulatus*" in ink, with an apparent pencil line drawn through *adamanteus*.

USNM 5021 and 5027 were logged into the Smithsonian Institution catalog on 30 January 1861, having been received from Dr. B. J. D. Irwin. The catalog indicated that USNM 5021 consisted of the head only of "*Crotalus lucifer*" from "Arizona". USNM 5027 was recorded as two specimens of "*Crotalus lepturus*" from "Fort Buchanan, Arizona", with the additional notation "1 Philad." entered under "Remarks." Specimen catalogs were not started in Philadelphia until about 1894 and show ANSP 7069 as "*Caudisona scutulata* Kennicott 1861" with the additional notation that it was originally one of

Smithsonian Institution. Washington, D. C.

United States 5021 National Museum.

Crotalus adamanteus scutulatus,

Ft Buchanan. Dr. Irwin.

Smithsonian Institution.

Older faded specimen tag (above) and the newer tag (below) from the jar containing USNM 5027. Photos: Steve Gotte and James Poindexter II, Smithsonian Institution; reprinted with permission from *Proceedings of the Biological Society of Washington* 126:11–16 (2013).

Current Number.	Original Number.	Name.	Sex.	Locality.
5026		Diadophis punctatus		Sta Cruz Ft. Buchanan Arizona
7		CROTALUS SCUTULATUS ~~Caudisona lepidurus~~		"

Collected by	Prepared by	Cost.	When entered.	No. of Specimens.	Remarks.
Dr. J.B.D. Irwin			Jan 30 1861	1	1 Phila.
"			"	2	REID. L.M. Klauber 1 Philad.

Portions of facing pages (above and below) of the Smithsonian Institution specimen catalog bearing the entry for USNM 5027 on 30 January 1861. The pencil note presumably resulted from Laurence Klauber's 1934 visit. Photos: Steve Gotte and James Poindexter II, Smithsonian Institution.

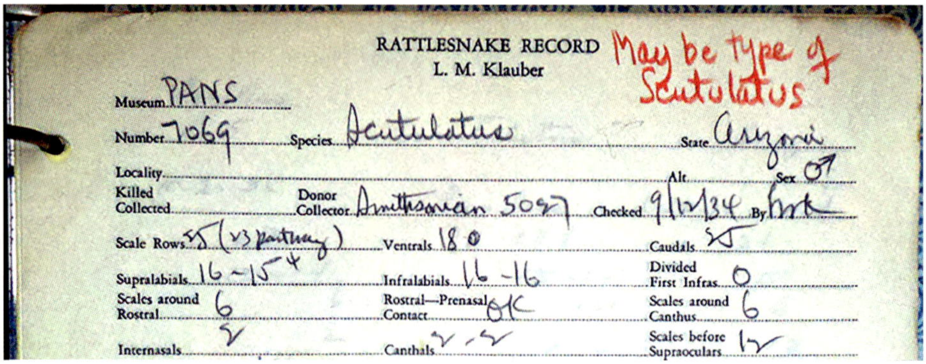

Top of Laurence Klauber's handwritten data sheet for ANSP (aka PANS) 7069. From the Archives of the Research Library, San Diego Natural History Museum.

two specimens comprising USNM 5027 at the Smithsonian. As described in Chapter 1, adding the surname of the original author to the italicized genus and species is the convention in taxonomy.

In those early days of discovering, classifying, and naming the creatures being collected in western North America, the taxonomy of many organisms was in constant flux. Some taxonomists lumped all the rattlesnakes with diamond-shaped dorsal markings together, including those we recognize today as *Crotalus atrox* (the western diamond-backed rattlesnake), *C. adamanteus* (the eastern diamond-backed rattlesnake), and *C. scutulatus*. The name from the 1861 Smithsonian catalogue entry, "*Crotalus lepturus*," was never published. The pencil line through "*adamanteus*" on the more recent specimen tag undoubtedly reflects a taxonomic revision in those early unsettled days.

Along with Klauber's collection of preserved animals, the San Diego Natural History Museum also curates Klauber's many diaries and field notes, as well as data sheets from his examinations of preserved specimens. Klauber's personal records indicate that he borrowed preserved rattlesnakes from the Smithsonian Institution on several occasions. A batch of rattlesnakes shipped to Klauber in September 1928 included USNM 5021 and 5027. His notes from examining those specimens reflect his comments in the footnote of *Rattlesnakes*: USNM 5021 is the wrong species but USNM 5027 is a "*scutulatus*," although it does not match Kennicott's description.

Then, in September 1934, Klauber traveled by train from San Diego to visit the major collections in the northeastern United States, including both the Academy of Natural Sciences in Philadelphia and the Smithsonian Institution in Washington, D.C. As far as I can determine from Klauber's records, this was the only time he examined ANSP 7069. Concerning Cope's identification of USNM 5021 as the type specimen, Klauber subsequently wrote in his notes,

"5027 is probably what he meant, but the USNM specimen doesn't agree with the description. The one at PANS does." At the top of the data sheet created by Klauber on 12 September 1934 for ANSP (aka PANS) 7069, he wrote in large red letters, "May be type of *scutulatus*."

However, despite Klauber's meticulous attention to detail, he inexplicably failed to mention ANSP 7069 in any of his many subsequent publications. In science, we often joke that you can never have too much data, for large numerical data sets yield more robust statistical results. Yet it is easy to lose information in a large volume of handwritten notes. After several trips to San Diego to peruse the notes, diaries, and the 200 three-ring binders containing Klauber's data sheets at the Natural History Museum, I found ANSP 7069 mentioned as the type specimen of the Mohave rattlesnake in only the two places noted here. I can only conclude that Klauber forgot about ANSP 7069 during the quarter century between his trip to Philadelphia and the preparation of *Rattlesnakes*. While it may be that a scientist can never have too much numerical data, one apparently can have too many notes, especially before computers were available to sort and search them.

Working with Ned Gilmore at ANSP, we verified John Cadle's determination that ANSP 7069 is consistent with Kennicott's original 1861 description. In 2013, we published "Type specimens of *Crotalus scutulatus* (Chordata: Reptilia: Squamata: Viperidae) re-examined, with new evidence after more than a century of confusion" in the *Proceedings of The Biological Society of Washington*, coauthored by me and my colleagues at the Smithsonian Institution and the Academy of Natural Sciences of Philadelphia. (Cardwell et al., 2013)

THE "TYPE LOCATION" – WHERE WAS THE FIRST ONE FOUND?

In our 2013 publication, we were also able to re-designate the type location for the Mohave rattlesnake as Fort Buchanan, Arizona. A type location is the place from which the type specimen was collected and is intended to represent a snapshot of the range and habitat of the species. Hobart Smith and Edward Taylor were first to publish Wickenburg, Arizona, as the type location in 1950 but their stated source for that determination does not contain supporting data. (Smith and Taylor, 1945:194 and 1950:353; see also Cardwell et al., 2013 for more details)

Dr. Bernard J. D. Irwin was an Army assistant surgeon posted to Fort Buchanan from December 1857 to July 1861. Many Army surgeons assigned to those early explorations of the American West also served as naturalists, collecting all sorts of natural history specimens which they preserved and shipped to the Smithsonian Institution (which provided containers and other supplies, as well as instructions). Dr. Irwin actually had an interest in rattlesnakes and their bites and was a particularly prolific collector, as is mentioned in the *Report of the Board of Regents of the Smithsonian Institution* in both 1860 and 1861. Fort Buchanan was established on the north bank of Sonoita Creek in 1857, in what is now Santa Cruz County in southern Arizona, and was abandoned and burned when the Civil War broke out (Fahey, 2017). Its ruins are located just west of the present-day town of Sonoita, very close to the Hog Canyon Road exit on State Highway 82. As it turns out, Cope's 1900 identification of Fort Buchanan as the origin of the type specimen was accurate, although he identified the wrong snake and mislabeled it.

Madrean Evergreen Woodland habitat is home to Mohave rattlesnakes near the town of Sonoita and the ruins of Fort Buchanan in Santa Cruz County, Arizona.

Interestingly, Dr. Irwin went on to distinguish himself in February 1861 when he led a rescue party through snow for nearly 100 miles from Fort Buchanan to Apache Pass to care for soldiers injured in a fight with Cochise. Some accounts of the Apache Pass conflict, known as the "Bascom Affair," are less than complimentary of the Army and the incident is said to have triggered The Apache Wars (1861-1886). But what makes Dr. Irwin's participation noteworthy is that, as a result of his efforts at Apache Pass, the collector of the first Mohave rattlesnake was awarded the Congressional Medal of Honor, our country's highest military award. Dr. Irwin retired from the Army a few months after receiving the CMH and was promoted to major general after retirement in 1904. He died in 1917 at the age of 87. Today, Irwin Army Hospital at Fort Riley, Kansas, is named in his honor (Fahey, 2015).

Venom being extracted from a Mohave rattlesnake.

Venom and Deadliness 5

Rattlesnakes produce some of the most complex venoms found in the animal kingdom (Mackessy, 2008; Mackessy and Castoe, 2016) and much of the urban legend surrounding Mohave rattlesnakes is due to the belief that their venom is particularly deadly. Although greatly exaggerated, this reputation has a legitimate origin in the standard LD_{50} toxicology tests that have been repeated by multiple researchers over the years (early results summarized by Glenn and Straight, 1982).

LD_{50} TESTS

"LD" is an abbreviation for "lethal dose" and LD_{50} tests are designed to find the dose of a particular venom that kills 50% of the test animals, a value known as the "median lethal dose." Test animals are usually laboratory mice, although other animals like rabbits and pigeons have sometimes been used. In such trials, test animals are divided into lots of equal numbers, often about 5–6 animals per lot, and the animals in each lot are given injections of an identical dose of venom. Each dose is measured in units of venom per unit of body mass and injections of individual animals are carefully scaled in proportion to the weight of the animal. In that way, the effect of small differences in size between test animals is minimized. Then, after waiting twenty-four hours (or some other specified period of time), the percentage of dead mice in each lot is

Species	LD_{50} Values (mg/kg)
Mohave Rattlesnake (Venom-A)	0.15
Midget Faded Rattlesnake	0.20
Tropical American Rattlesnake	0.20
Eastern Diamondback Rattlesnake	2.70
Mohave Rattlesnake (Venom-B)	3.50
Western Diamondback Rattlesnake	4.50

Median Lethal Dose (LD_{50}) values for several rattlesnake species tested in mice, including venom-A and venom-B Mohave rattlesnakes. Adapted from Glenn and Straight, 1978.

computed. With a little trial and error, the dose that kills 50% of the mice – the LD_{50} value – is determined. This test has been widely used by toxinologists to rank the lethality of all kinds of substances, including many animal poisons and venoms.

Most populations of Mohave rattlesnakes produce venom containing a potent neurotoxin that usually yields a lower LD_{50} value than the venoms of other North American pitvipers. That is, it takes less venom from Mohave rattlesnakes than from other species to kill mice. And compared to most other species, it takes a lot less.

VARIATION IN MOHAVE RATTLESNAKE VENOM

The neurotoxin produced by Mohave rattlesnakes was named "Mojave toxin" by Allan Bieber and his colleagues in 1975 (Bieber et al., 1975). But soon thereafter, Glenn and Straight (1978) identified a large area in southcentral Arizona where Mohave rattlesnake venom contains no Mojave toxin, instead producing lots of local tissue injury but little or no neurotoxicity, similar to most other kinds of rattlesnakes. They labeled Mohave rattlesnake venom containing Mojave toxin "venom-A" and venom without Mojave toxin "venom-B."

Bites to people by venom-A Mohaves produce symptoms that can include fatigue, low blood pressure, drooping eyelids, and difficulty speaking and swallowing. In more serious cases, diaphragm function – and thus respiration – may be compromised (Smith and Bush, 2010).

Furthermore, venom-A bites usually cause little or no local tissue damage (i.e., pain, swelling, bruising, tissue death) which is common following bites by many other rattlesnake species, as well as by venom-B Mohave rattlesnakes.

Our understanding of the distribution of venom-A and venom-B populations was further enhanced by Wilkinson et al. (1991), who found some animals on the margin between venom-A and venom-B populations that produce "venom-A+B," meaning the venom contains both Mojave toxin and tissue-destroying components. More recently, research by Dan Massey et al. (2012) demonstrated a gradation of Mohave rattlesnake venom components across southern Arizona, with venom containing tissue-destroying metalloproteinase but lacking Mojave toxin in southcentral Arizona but shifting to venom rich in Mojave toxin without significant tissue-destroying enzymes in southeastern Arizona and adjacent New Mexico. Note the lack of a well-defined boundary between venom-A and -B populations in Arizona (map, next page).

At the time this book is being prepared, new genetic and venom protein studies of Mohave rattlesnakes from throughout their range by Jason

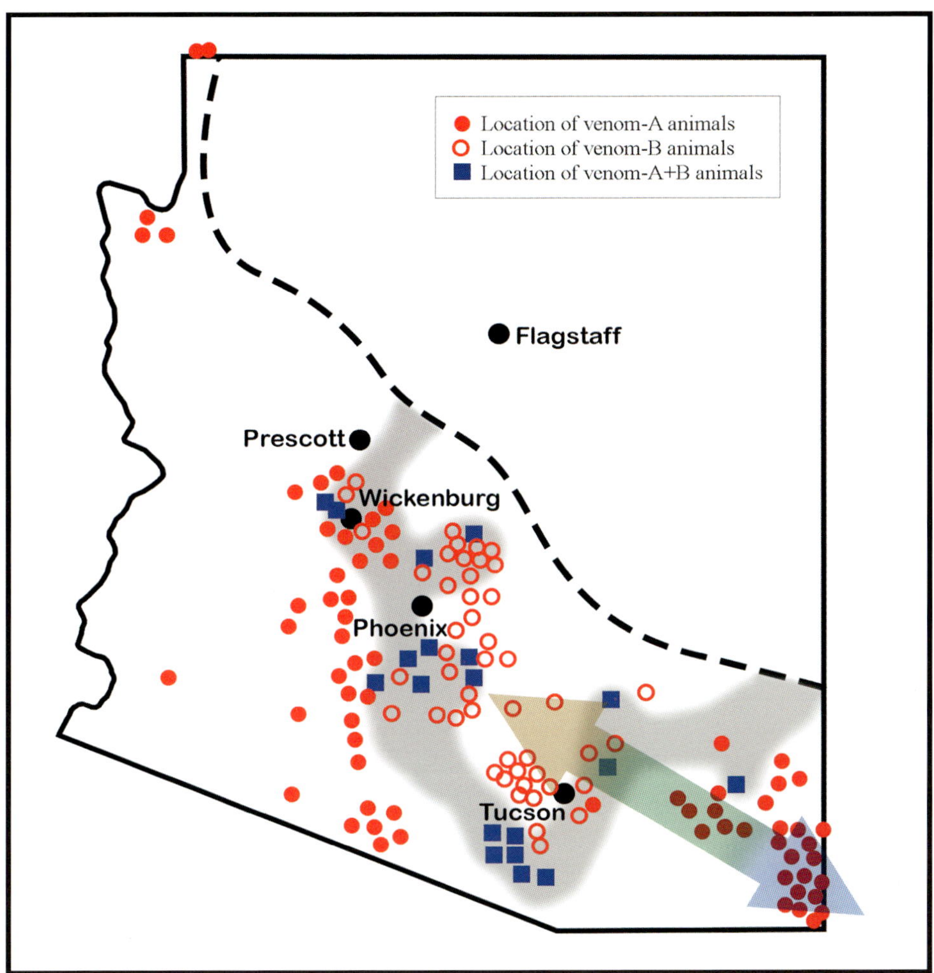

Distribution of Mohave rattlesnake venom components in Arizona. Large dashed line: approximate margin of Mohave rattlesnake distribution. Filled red circles: venom-A specimens; open red circles: venom-B specimens; blue squares: venom-A+B specimens; gray shaded area: approximate intergradation zone between venom-A and venom-B. Colored arrow indicates gradation of venom components in southeastern Arizona; brown: venom dominated by metalloproteinase without Mojave toxin; green: Mojave toxin with myotoxin; blue: Mojave toxin without myotoxin or metalloproteinase. Adapted from Wilkinson et al. (1991) and Massey et al. (2012). Reprinted from *Rattlesnakes of Arizona*, Vol. 1 (2016).

Strickland and his colleagues (Strickland et al., 2018) provide evidence that other venom-B populations exist in the Chihuahuan Desert and on the Central Mexican Plateau. As in Arizona, borders between venom-A and venom-B populations are not well-defined and venom-A+B animals are present but relatively rare. To date, Mohave rattlesnakes sampled in California, Utah and Texas have all produced venom-A. However, an unusual snakebite case in California by a verified Mohave rattlesnake that produced neurotoxicity plus serious systemic bleeding (Bush et al., 2012) indicates that venom-A+B (and potentially venom-B) animals can occasionally occur anywhere within the species' range.

Other recent findings include analyses by Giulia Zancolli and her colleagues (Zancolli et al., 2019) indicating that, despite the blurred boundary in southern Arizona between venom-A and venom-B populations, the venom types within these populations appear to be stable. That is, neither venom type is spreading into the other population, despite genetic evidence of constant gene flow between them.

The most likely explanation is that there are different selective pressures favoring each venom type on opposite sides of the intergrade zone – and we have not yet teased out those factors.

"TOXIC" vs. "TENDERIZING" VENOMS

Steve Mackessy, one of the world's leading authorities on the biochemistry of snake venoms, describes this fundamental difference in snake venoms another way: "toxicity vs. tenderizers." Among the rattlesnakes, venoms with high levels of neurotoxins are particularly deadly in mouse LD_{50} studies, while venoms rich in tissue-destroying proteases are far less efficient mouse killers.

Most interesting is the discovery that venoms containing a lot of neurotoxin have very little tissue-destroying metalloproteinase and vice versa, hence categorizing them as either "toxic" or "tenderizing" venoms (Mackessy, 2010a).

You may wonder why all species don't have neurotoxic venoms and what good are the tenderizers? To be sure, snake venoms are far more complex than just neurotoxins and proteases. Some of the other components are "myotoxins" – a family of enzymes that attack muscle tissue. Myotoxins are well represented in most neurotoxic and tenderizing venoms and are likely the most important venom component for incapacitating prey animals bitten by snakes without much neurotoxin. The value of tissue-destroying proteases, on the other hand, is theorized to aid digestion, particularly at cool temperatures (summarized by Mackessy, 2010b). Another class of proteins called "disintegrins" has been implicated in recent years in chemically "tagging" a bitten prey animal, allowing the snake to scent-trail it after the strike.

WHY HAVE TWO KINDS OF VENOM?

One final interesting development from recent Mohave rattlesnake venom research concerns how Mojave toxin is distributed across a hybrid zone. Studies are being focused on the one known hybrid zone where venom-A Mohave rattlesnakes have been shown by compelling genetic evidence to have been interbreeding for many generations with another rattlesnake species that relies on tenderizing venom. While first generation hybrids usually produce both Mojave toxin and tissue-destroying metalloproteinase, Mojave toxin has not spread into the other rattlesnake population away from the hybrid zone. (Zancolli et al., 2016, 2019)

Natural selection theory suggests that these different venom types should be competing and whichever one is most efficient should slowly replace the less efficient type. And while some experts have voiced confusion that this does not appear to be happening, there is a simple explanation: selective pressures on opposite sides of the hybrid zone must be different and favor tenderizers in one area and neurotoxin in the other – just like the interface between venom-A and -B Mohaves. The real question is what are those selection pressures? Many of us believe it is likely diet and/or foraging behavior but that remains to be determined. Find more information and references in Chapter 6 – Hybrids.

THE LAST WORD ABOUT VENOM – ARE YOU A MAN OR A MOUSE?

So, in the language of toxinologists, "toxicity" means "lethality." And it is certainly true that decades of research reveals that venom-A Mohave rattlesnakes are far more deadly than most other snakes… to laboratory mice! But do those results translate well to human snakebite victims?

Mohave rattlesnakes are widely distributed and are often locally common where they occur. Second only to western diamondbacks in frequency of human encounters in Arizona and west Texas, they are easily the most often encountered rattlesnake in the heavily populated Mohave Desert communities of California, where western diamondbacks are absent. As a result, Mohave rattlesnakes are responsible for a significant proportion of the hundreds of rattlesnake bites treated every year by hospitals in these areas, yet fatalities are rare.

While it is often difficult to reliably determine the species of snake responsible for a bite after a patient arrives at a hospital, we know that venomous snakes in general kill only about five or six people annually throughout the United States (Forrester et al., 2018) and many of those deaths happen in places where there are no Mohave rattlesnakes. For example, over the past couple of decades in California (the area with which I am most familiar), the tiny handful of snakebite deaths that occurred happened in non-desert areas where only the western rattlesnake (*Crotalus oreganus*) is found, despite dozens of Mohave rattlesnake bites being treated annually in Los Angeles, San Bernardino and Kern Counties.

In fact, I should note that experts estimate (there is no standardized method to collect these data) that there are about 8,000 venomous snakebites each year in the United States (Norris, Bush and Cardwell, 2015), making the tiny number of fatalities equivalent to less than 1 in 1,000. In other words, more than 99.9% of U.S. snakebite victims survive!

Probably due to the particularly high number of well-recognized snakebite experts in southern Arizona over many decades – as well as lots of rattlesnakes – we have some of the best hard data on snakebites from an area where Mohave rattlesnakes are common. The late Dr. David Hardy Sr., a physician and avid herpetologist, reported in 1983 on 15 bites in Arizona by Mohave rattlesnakes where he was able to personally confirm the species (Hardy, 1983). These cases, treated in eight hospitals in Tucson, Phoenix, and Wickenburg between 1975 and 1982, produced no deaths. Furthermore, in a retrospective study of 159 snakebite patients in the Tucson area between 1973 and 1980 (Hardy, 1983, 1985), Hardy estimated that 50% were western diamondback bites and 30% were Mohave bites, yet no fatalities resulted.

In nine cases in which "snakebite" was listed as the cause of death on Arizona death certificates between 1969 and 1984, two could be attributed to Mohave rattlesnakes. Interestingly, both were captive snakes and the bitten owners never sought medical attention, both dying at home within 7–8 hours, presumably from "complications of hypotension" (low blood pressure), per Hardy (1986).

In their more recent study of the geographic variation of Mohave rattlesnake venom, Massey et al. (2012) reviewed 516 rattlesnake bite cases occurring from 2002 to 2009 in Arizona's Pima and Cochise Counties, which produced only one fatality. While these bites represented various rattlesnake species, they undoubtedly included a significant number of Mohave rattlesnake bites.

I am not suggesting that Mohave rattlesnake bites are not serious medical emergencies – and even potentially deadly, just that they are not nearly as frequently deadly as many field guides and medical references would lead us to believe. Indeed, a 63-year-old woman succumbed in October 2007 following a confirmed Mohave rattlesnake bite in Yavapai County, Arizona. According to fire department and coroner records, she collapsed while on the phone with the 9-1-1 operator and was treated by paramedics within a few minutes but

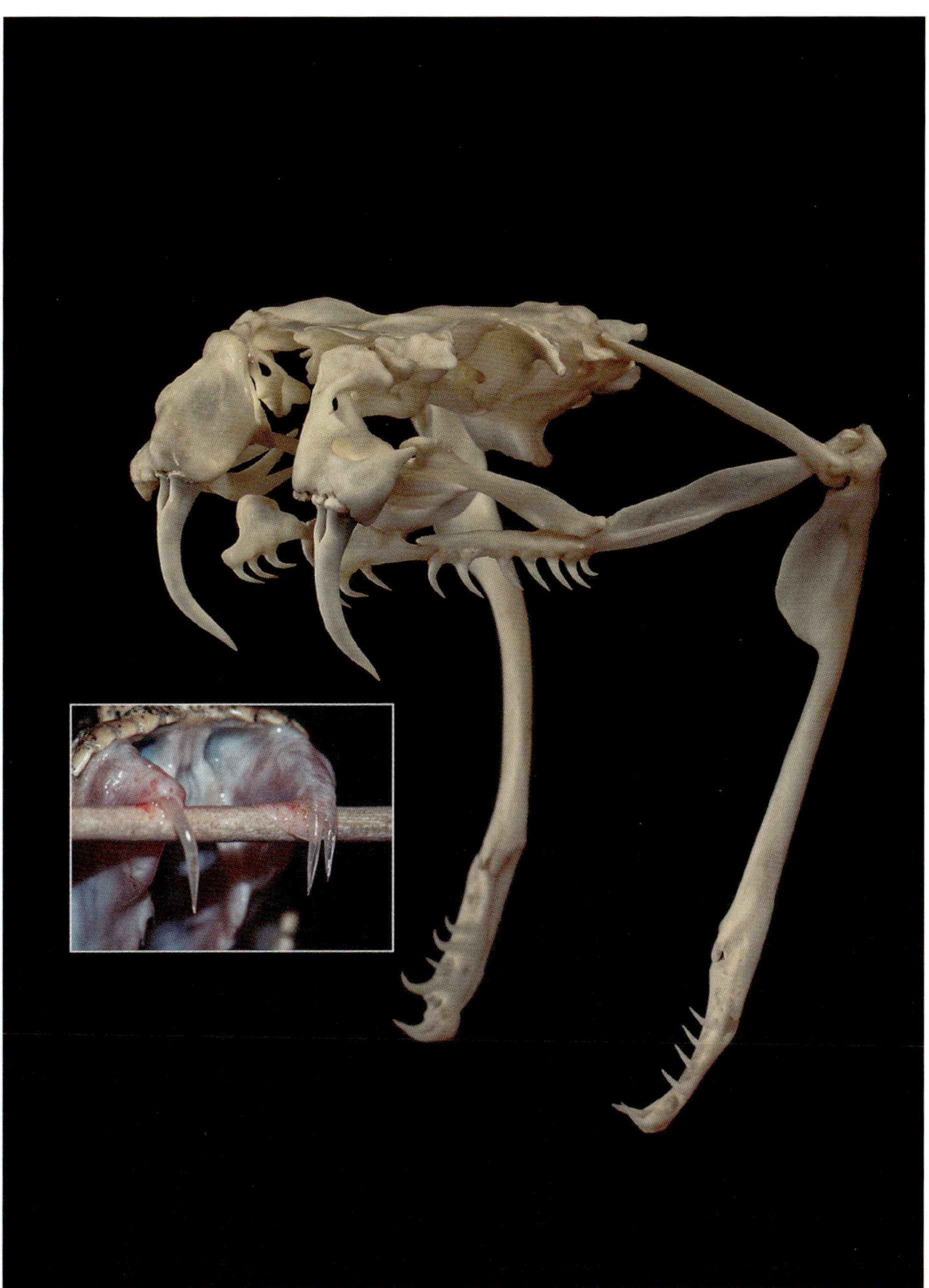

Rattlesnake fangs are slender, hollow, and sharp, but less than ¼-inch long in all but the largest animals. They remain folded against the roof of the mouth except during a bite or when swallowing prey. Fangs are replaced periodically, briefly producing a double fang (inset), until the older fang loosens and is lost – usually swallowed with prey. Developing replacement fangs are visible in this skull, behind the erect ones.

had suffered an apparent acute allergic reaction immediately following the bite. Thus, it is likely that her bite was survivable except for a separate cascade of immunological responses that were simply set in motion by the snakebite.

Similarly, a well-known Arizona physician and herpetologist was reportedly killed in August 1965 by a Mohave rattlesnake bite near Klondyke, in Graham County, Arizona. Snakebite expert Dr. Fred Shannon lapsed into unconsciousness almost immediately after the bite and succumbed about 36 hours later, according to newspaper accounts and an obituary in a herpetological journal (Anonymous, 1965; Smith and Russell, 1965). Unlike the recent Yavapai County victim, Dr. Shannon reportedly had a history of previous rattlesnake bites that could have rendered him susceptible to an acute allergic reaction in the event of a future bite. Since quick incapacitation by rattlesnake venom, including that of Mohave rattlesnakes, is extraordinarily rare, it is likely that both of these victims were killed by an acute allergic response to the foreign protein (e.g., an anaphylactic or anaphylactoid reaction), rather than by the primary effects of the venom.

I have been working with and around rattlesnakes – and particularly Mohave rattlesnakes – for half a century, including conducting the first-ever long-term radiotelemetry study of wild Mohave rattlesnakes that documented more than 3,700 close encounters. I have also studied and eventually taught and lectured on snakebite avoidance and first aid for many years. Given all that experience, if I had to choose a rattlesnake species to be bitten by, I would prefer it be a venom-A Mohave rattlesnake!

Why, you ask? Because most other rattlesnakes can cause horrible tissue damage around the bite, as well as life-threatening systemic problems like spontaneous bleeding, kidney failure, etc. This damage begins immediately following the bite and can worsen until antivenom therapy is well underway. On the other hand, a venom-A Mohave bite will likely produce little or no tissue damage and the neurotoxic effects generally do not become incapacitating for several hours – allowing time to get to a hospital and antivenom. And while modern antivenoms can arrest the progression of injury caused by both venom types, it cannot repair damage already done by the "tenderizing" venoms before reaching medical help. Antivenom does, however, reverse the neurotoxic effects of Mojave toxin, leaving no long-term disability.

But make no mistake… a Mohave rattlesnake bite is a dangerous injury! Unusual effects do occasionally occur and we know that venom-B or venom-A+B snakes can be encountered in unexpected populations. And, if you have been exposed to rattlesnake venom before (as I have), even just by inhalation of minute amounts of dried venom, you may experience an immediate life-threatening allergic reaction to a future bite. Finally, regardless of the kind of

A wild Mohave rattlesnake eating a Merriam's kangaroo rat (*Dipodomys merriami*).

The tapered rattle of this Mohave rattlesnake identifies it as a young adult. Since young rattlesnakes grow rapidly, each new rattle segment is wider that the last and the original "birth button" forms the pointed end.

snake, the antivenom bill alone will do long-term damage to your finances! So snakebite prevention is far more preferable than first aid and treatment. Nonetheless, the bottom line is this:

Mohaves are the deadliest of rattlesnakes – only if you're a lab mouse!

Hybrid Mohave Rattlesnakes 6

Rumors about Mohave rattlesnakes being some sort of recent hybrid hold a prominent place in Mohave green folklore. I heard the most dramatic claim in the 1990s during a radio interview in Victorville, California, when a listener called in to tell me – and the radio audience – that Mohave greens are a new hyper-venomous hybrid created from green mambas intentionally bred with some non-venomous species by the U.S. government to put down enemy tunnels in Viet Nam. When that war ended, the excess snakes were released at Fort Irwin, near Barstow, California, and that's why Mohave greens were unheard of before 1975!

Yes, that phone call really happened!

HISTORICAL ACCOUNTS

Natural hybrids of any species are intriguing for a variety of biological reasons, but hybridization in Mohave rattlesnakes is particularly noteworthy because of the abundant folklore. Contributing to the popular belief that Mohaves readily hybridize with other snakes are the popular field guides to western reptiles and amphibians authored by Robert Stebbins, in which he states unequivocally (1985:232; 2003:416) that Mohave rattlesnakes hybridize with southern Pacific rattlesnakes in the western Antelope Valley of Los Angeles County, California.

Indeed, rumors of peculiar-looking rattlesnakes abound in this western-most tip of the Mohave Desert. Having lived nearby and hearing the stories for many years, yet never seeing what I thought was a strange-looking rattlesnake, I corresponded with Dr. Stebbins several times and spoke to him once about the origin of this information. While he could not recall what prompted him to suggest such hybrids, he encouraged me to search his field notes and correspondence archived in the Grinnell-Miller Library at U.C. Berkeley's Museum of Vertebrate Zoology. Although I have done so twice, I have been unable to find any related information. In his last field guide, Stebbins and coauthor Samuel McGinnis (2012:416) altered the claim a bit, stating that the range of the western rattlesnake (*Crotalus oreganus*, which includes the southern Pacific rattlesnake) "may only slightly overlap" with Mohave rattlesnakes “where some presumed hybrids have been found.” They offered no further explanation for the claim and Stebbins died the following year.

Dr. Stebbins was a beloved educator, a highly-respected herpetologist and, for many years, curator of herpetology at U.C. Berkeley’s Museum of Vertebrate Zoology. I have no doubt that there was some tangible basis for his original 1985 claim of hybrid Mohave rattlesnakes in Antelope Valley. But that was before scientists could easily compare DNA and such determinations were made almost exclusively from comparison of visible characters. Ultimately, neither he nor I were ever able to resurrect the origin of that hybrid claim.

Interestingly, Laurence Klauber made the following observation long ago:

> “In California, intergradation between *scutulatus* and *oreganus* might be expected in the Tehachapi Mountains northwest of Antelope Valley or the San Gabriel and San Bernardino Ranges southwest of the desert. Yet notwithstanding considerable available material no intergrades as yet have been forthcoming” (Klauber, 1930:121)

Klauber’s personal notes (archived at SDNHM) contain a description of a series of Mohave rattlesnakes and western rattlesnakes collected in 1933 from the edge the Mohave Desert at the foot of the Tehachapi Mountains “20 miles north of Mohave” in Kern County, California, which Klauber compared for evidence of hybridization but found none.

Price (2009) commented that Mohave rattlesnakes and western diamondbacks hybridize in the Big Bend region of Texas but he did not supply supporting data. But according to Conant (1975:237) and Conant and Collins (1998:412), “Mojave Rattlesnakes in western Texas are often aberrant and one or more identification characters may approximate those of Western Diamondback.” In other words, they are easily confused.

Jacob (1977) evaluated the possibility of hybridization between Mohave rattlesnakes and western diamondbacks in areas where they are found together using physical and molecular methods and concluded that they were not hybridizing. Another study described in more detail below (Murphy and Crabtree, 1988) looked for genetic evidence of hybridization with western diamondbacks in west Texas without success. And in their recent investigation of potential hybridization between Mohaves and prairie rattlesnakes in southwestern New Mexico, Zancolli et al. (2016) also included western diamondbacks in their analyses because they are also common in the study area, yet no evidence of hybridization involving diamondbacks was found.

Wild Mohave x prairie rattlesnake (*Crotalus scutulatus* x *viridis*) hybrids from Hidalgo County, New Mexico. This is the only known well-established wild population of hybrid Mohaves. Photos courtesy of Wolfgang Wüster.

HYBRIDIZATION IN CAPTIVITY

Rattlesnakes occasionally hybridize in captivity, when animals of different species are caged together in unnatural conditions. Apparently reliable accounts have been published of Mohave rattlesnakes producing offspring in captivity with several other species of *Crotalus*. Many of these accounts contain photographs of the offspring and some report babies preserved in museum collections.

HYBRIDIZATION AMONG WILD MOHAVE RATTLESNAKES

If captive rattlesnake hybrids are scarce, compelling evidence of wild hybrids is rare and examples involving Mohave rattlesnakes are nearly nonexistent – with one very significant exception. In 1990, venom researchers Jim Glenn and Richard Straight analyzed 113 venom samples from 46 populations of prairie rattlesnakes (*Crotalus viridis*) for evidence of Mojave toxin, as a potential indicator of wild hybridization with Mohave rattlesnakes (Glenn and Straight, 1990). Fourteen of their samples were from southwestern New Mexico and three of those tested positive for Mojave toxin. These three animals were identical in appearance to typical prairie rattlesnakes and the researchers reported that their results "strongly suggest" that the samples containing Mojave toxin were evidence of "some previous hybridization" with Mohave rattlesnakes. However, Mojave toxin-like venom components are known to be produced by a number of other rattlesnakes not suspected to be hybrids, including some very closely related to prairie rattlesnakes. Nonetheless, recent genetic and biochemical evidence produced by Giulia Zancolli, Wolfgang Wüster and their colleagues, provides compelling support for Glenn and Straight's (1990) conclusion.

Zancolli and her colleagues aggressively sampled Mohave rattlesnakes and prairie rattlesnakes in southwestern New Mexico and found abundant evidence of long-term hybridization well beyond occasional first-generation offspring (Zancolli et al., 2016). Though the hybrid zone is small, their analyses provides compelling genetic evidence of multi-generational "back-crosses," meaning that first-generation hybrids have successfully produced their own fertile offspring, including from pairings with pure-bred mates, thus thoroughly mixing the genes from the two species. Given that cross-species hybridization often results in significant disability – frequently including infertility due to mismatches between the chromosomes, the success of this natural Mohave rattlesnake x prairie rattlesnake hybrid zone is consistent with the close evolutionary relationship between these species, as previously described by phylogeneticists.

Other evidence of wild Mohave hybrids is very scarce. Over the years, I have examined only two museum specimens that I believe were wild Mohave rattlesnake hybrids. One is catalogued as "*C. scutulatus* x *viridis*" (Mohave x prairie rattlesnake) at the Museum of Vertebrate Zoology at U. C. Berkeley (specimen #MVZ 209127). It was collected as a road-kill in 1988 in the vicinity of the Zancolli et al. (2016) study area and bears some odd-looking scale arrangements. When I examined it in 2005, I concluded that its appearance was not inconsistent with the natural variation I had come to expect among Mohave rattlesnakes. However, after the compelling evidence found by Zancolli, et al. (2016) in the same area, I now suspect that this animal could be a hybrid.

The other museum specimen I believe to be a wild Mohave hybrid is in the collection of the Los Angeles County Museum of Natural History (specimen #LACM 130808). It is catalogued as a Mohave rattlesnake, collected as a road-kill in 1979 near the US-Mexico border southwest of the town of Sierra Blanca in West Texas. Although this animal looked generally like a typical Mohave rattlesnake, an unusual arrangement of head scales and odd genetic results attracted the attention of biologists Robert Murphy and Ben Crabtree. They compared thirteen locations in the DNA that typically differ between Mohave, prairie and western diamondback rattlesnakes, all of which inhabit the area where LACM 130808 was collected, and found that at every location on a chromosome where prairie and Mohave rattlesnakes differ, this animal had a "heterozygote," meaning that the paternal and maternal copies of these genes were different – one consistent with a prairie rattlesnake and the other with a Mohave. The only reasonable explanation was that the animal was a first-generation hybrid (Murphy and Crabtree, 1988).

It is worth noting that Giuilia Zancolli and her colleagues also sampled this West Texas area nearly thirty years later for evidence of hybridization between Mohave and prairie rattlesnakes without success, indicating that the hybrid animal identified by Murphy and Crabtree is probably not part of a well-established hybrid population like the one Zancolli and her colleagues discovered in southwestern New Mexico.

There have been a handful of provocative photos of live rattlesnakes published in print and posted online over the years, with morphological traits suggestive of intergrades between Mohave rattlesnakes and other species. Other authors have also commented on photos of apparent hybrids (e.g., Campbell and Lamar, 2004:484) but without background data or the animals in hand, hard evidence is lacking. While we know that natural variation accounts for many differences in pattern, color and other traits within pure-bred populations, it is probably naïve to think that undetected wild hybridization involving Mohave rattlesnakes never occurs. Yet evidence available today suggests that wild

At first glance, this animal looks like a Mohave rattlesnake – until the tail comes into view. Plus, the top of the head is covered with tiny scales and there are four internasal scales in contact with the rostral, all diagnostic traits of a western rattlesnake. It was photographed at the base of the Sierra Nevada Mountains in Kern County, California, where westerns and Mohaves are likely in contact. Is it just a greenish western rattlesnake? Photos by Alice Abela.

hybrids are quite rare outside of the small area in southwestern New Mexico. And remembering that Mohave and prairie rattlesnakes are closely related, the chances of a wild hybrid with a more distantly related species being healthy, fertile and successful enough for those genes to endure and even spread back into one or both species seems unlikely.

This specimen, tagged UAZ 40162, has been sitting in a jar of alcohol in the University of Arizona Museum of Natural History for more than four decades, where it is labeled as a prairie x Mohave rattlesnake hybrid. Although it was collected about 40 miles north of the hybrid zone documented by Zancolli et al. (2016), note the color of the tail rings and three internasals touching the rostral. Sadly, the process of "fixing" these older specimens in formalin before storing them in alcohol without first harvesting a tissue sample causes DNA to become cross-linked with proteins and has so far prevented later genetic analysis.

A typical Mohave rattlesnake basking at dawn. Contrary to popular belief, snakes do not relish high temperatures. In fact, they tolerate cool temperatures well but getting too hot can be quickly lethal. On hot days, rattlesnakes usually take shelter underground.

Population Status and Conservation

7

POPULATION STATUS

Most, if not all, Mohave rattlesnake populations are likely healthy and stable where they are undisturbed by human activities. In fact, the International Union for Conservation of Nature (IUCN) lists the Mohave rattlesnake as a "species of least concern" on the current IUCN Red List of Threatened Species (www.iucnredlist.org).

Unlike some other rattlesnakes that are adapted to specialized isolated habitats like high elevation talus slopes, alpine forests, and rocky desert hillsides, Mohave rattlesnakes occupy very large, relatively flat, interconnected tracts of land covered with a variety of soil types and plant communities. They are wide-spread inhabitants of the Mohave, Sonoran and Chihuahuan Deserts, each of which has a unique climate and ecology, plus grassland habitats and juniper-covered foothills. In areas they share with the ubiquitous western diamondback, Mohave rattlesnakes are usually the next most encountered

As human development encroaches into rattlesnake habitat, encounters between people and rattlesnakes that usually don't end well for the rattlesnakes become inevitable. In particular, cars take an enormous toll on all wildlife, including snakes like this large male Mohave rattlesnake.

rattlesnake after diamondbacks. Where there are no diamondbacks within their range, Mohaves are typically the most abundant rattlesnake.

Although diet analysis from my 2001-2004 field work in California revealed that kangaroo rats and pocket mice made up 75% of the diet of that population, they also ate several other kinds of rodents, plus a variety of lizards. I view Mohaves as dietary generalists, with some populations likely adapted to efficiently kill kangaroo rats but also feeding on any small vertebrate they can kill and swallow. My California study included the rainless year of 2002 and I found Mohave rattlesnakes to be well adapted to survive in very dry conditions, satisfying almost all of their water needs with the body water of their prey (Cardwell, 2013). While they will undoubtedly be vulnerable to our planet's warming climate, I suspect they will be able to initially endure the change, at least until their prey is adversely affected.

But human encroachment into rattlesnake habitat invariably results in local extermination of the rattlesnakes. Several factors are generally involved, including lethal encounters with automobiles, grading away natural habitat which destroys shelters for both rattlesnakes and their prey, and direct persecution by people when snakes are encountered.

CONSERVATION

Rattlesnake conservation has been a contentious issue in the United States for many years, with historic paranoia and maltreatment yielding very slowly to more common-sense attitudes. In addition to the frequent killing of individual rattlesnakes, huge numbers of rattlesnakes have been slaughtered in certain areas of the United States at "rattlesnake roundups," as well as by extermination campaigns targeting communal winter dens. However, Mohave rattlesnakes do not live where rattlesnake roundups occur and they do not invite mass extermination efforts by denning communally. Other than just being rattlesnakes, the only issue that draws extraordinary animosity from people is the Mohave rattlesnake's undeserved reputation for aggressiveness and unusually deadly venom.

LEGAL STATUS

Because they are widely distributed and very common in many parts of their range, Mohave rattlesnakes do not enjoy legally protected status federally or in any U. S. state except one. Utah lists Mohave rattlesnakes as a "wildlife species of concern" (Utah Sensitive Species List, updated 1 November 2017) because their distribution within the state is restricted to a tiny area in southern

This little guy is only a few days old. The milky tone to his eye, the whitish ring around the base of his first rattle segment, and the dry onionskin appearance of his body are all evidence that he has begun his postpartum ecdysis cycle, which will be completed about 7-10 days after birth.

Utah's Mohave Desert habitat that is being fragmented and destroyed by the expanding human population.

The Utah population of Mohave rattlesnakes results from the species' distribution barely extending across the state line onto Washington County's Beaver Dam Slope from Mohave County, Arizona, where the population is apparently robust. Nonetheless, the State of Utah prohibits the collection and possession of Mohave rattlesnakes, per Utah Wildlife Administrative Rule R657-53-28(c)(xiv). It is worthwhile to note that Utah protects all rattlesnake species, even those not included on the state's Sensitive Species List.

Arizona, California, Nevada, New Mexico, and Texas all permit Mohave rattlesnakes to be "taken" (captured, killed, or possessed dead or alive) with various license requirements and bag limits. As near as I can determine, Mexico does not protect relatively large widely-distributed rattlesnakes like Mohaves. While a few rattlesnake species are reportedly protected in some areas, I am told by colleagues who work in Mexico that enforcement of such regulations is not common.

Rattlesnakes are not territorial but males like these Mohaves will fight over access to a female. There is no biting during these bouts, only wrestling, and one will eventually tire and give up. Photo courtesy of Jeff Lemm.

Behavior and Ecology 8

This is a brief summary of what we know about the private lives of Mohave rattlesnakes. I have drawn largely on more than 3,700 close encounters with wild Mohaves during my 2001-2004 field study, as well as the published studies of others, new observations from my current field study, anecdotal observations by myself and many colleagues and numerous studies of preserved museum specimens. While I have endeavored to answer the most commonly-asked questions here, many more details can be found in my Mohave rattlesnake account in volume one of *Rattlesnakes of Arizona* (Cardwell, 2016), as well as other references listed below.

HABITAT

Within arid environments, I consider Mohave rattlesnakes to be habitat generalists. They are widely distributed across three very different deserts: the relatively dry and cold Mohave Desert, where most precipitation is produced by cold winter storms; the Sonoran Desert, with more complex biological communities produced by warmer winters with most rain coming from summer monsoons; and the Chihuahuan Desert, which is highest in elevation, more moist, and produces the most complex communities. While a great deal of its distribution occurs on desert valley floors and bajadas dominated by creosote bush and mesquite, Mohave rattlesnakes are also at home in grassland communities such as those found in southeastern Arizona and southwestern New Mexico, and even in pine-oak woodland like the southwestern foothills of Arizona's Mogollon Rim and Mexico's Central Plateau.

Klauber (1972) wrote that Mohave rattlesnakes "are not absent from rocky areas, but seem to have no particular need of rocks." This observation mirrors my own experience. I have never found Mohaves sheltering under rocks or using fissures in rock outcrops for shelter but they are frequently found on soil covered with pebbles and angular rock fragments washed down from the parent bedrock of distant hills. Wherever they occur, they seem to prefer relatively flat ground with sparse vegetation. And while they are often found on coarse, even rocky soil, they are rarely, if ever, found on rocky hillsides, as are many other species.

REPRODUCTION

The reproductive season for Mohave rattlesnakes is bimodal; that is, it occurs during two periods each year (Schuett, 1992; Schuett et al., 2002; Cardwell, 2008). Courtship and mating occurs in late summer and fall before being interrupted by cold weather (Aldridge and Duvall, 2002), after which reproductive behavior continues in the spring. There is little or no courtship during June and July. Although mating only occurs during two periods each year, males usually have sperm in their ducts year-around and females can store viable sperm for long periods (likely several years; Schuett, 1992), so it is possible for fertilization to occur in almost any season. Young are born alive in late summer, usually arriving in mid-August in Arizona's Sonoran Desert and in mid-September in the Mohave Desert with its shorter summer (Cardwell, 2008). Litter size varies between five and thirteen with an average of eight (Klauber, 1972). Female Mohaves cannot produce more than one brood per year and usually skip a year or more as they rebuild sufficient body fat to sustain another pregnancy.

All scaled reptiles are covered by a thin outer layer of skin that reduces evaporative water loss but does not grow with the animal. As a result, the snakes must replace this covering periodically, which happens more frequently when they are young and growing rapidly. This process, called "shedding" (the technical term is "ecdysis"), first happens about 7–10 days after rattlesnakes are born. Thanks to radiotelemetry, we know that postpartum females of most rattlesnake species remain with their kids until they shed the first time, after which mom and babies disperse to find food before they have to hibernate in a few weeks. As a result, baby rattlesnakes encountered by people are at least a week old.

Interestingly, my 40-month field study failed to document such maternal accompaniment in Mohave rattlesnakes. However, the pregnant females I radio-tracked during my original study all gave birth during a severe drought. Likely as a result of being water-stressed, they continued to hunt during pregnancy and may have delivered still-born young. In any event, they did not remain with their young and I never found the babies. I originally suspected that Mohaves might behave differently than other rattlesnakes with their young. But then in August 2016, Arizona herpetologist Marty Feldner photographed a female Mohave rattlesnake coiled a few inches in front of a rodent burrow with a newborn Mohave visible inside the burrow behind her. Based on that photo, it seems likely that Mohave moms remain with their kids after birth like other rattlesnakes and my early observations were skewed by the drought. My radiotelemetry study currently underway in southern Arizona should soon

A female Mohave rattlesnake delivering a brood of about eight babies.

settle this question. Mohave rattlesnakes reach sexual maturity at about 1½ years of age and 16 inches for males and in about two years and 24 inches for females. (Cardwell, 2008; Goldberg and Rosen, 2000).

PREDATORY BEHAVIOR AND DIET

Most rattlesnakes, including Mohaves, are ambush hunters. In other words, they seldom actively forage for their prey, as do gophersnakes, racers, and many other snakes. Instead, they prefer to sit-and-wait for prey to come within strike range, which is advantageous in their arid environment, allowing them to rely on anaerobic metabolism, conserving both energy and water while also reducing evaporation through the skin by remaining coiled most of the time. Their preferred ambush position is a flat, round "pancake coil." An alternative is what I call the "burrow entrance ambush position" or BEAP. BEAP involves the rattlesnake lying in the entrance to a rodent burrow with its body concealed in the burrow behind it. The neck is tightly re-curved, ready to propel the head out of the hole for a strike. Herpetologists believe that ambush locations are likely selected by detecting chemical traces of the prey or even the odor of a successful hunt by another rattlesnake. Once a prey animal wanders within strike range, rattlesnakes deliver a lightning-quick attack, propelling the head

Common Mohave rattlesnake ambush positions: a round "pancake" coil (top) and the burrow entrance ambush position or "BEAP" (bottom), just waiting for the burrow's occupant to return home.

forward by quickly straightening the neck and part of the body and injecting a lethal dose of venom with their hollow fangs.

Adult Mohave rattlesnakes eat mostly rodents which, with their big incisor teeth, are capable of inflicting serious injury to the snake. As a result, rattlesnakes typically strike, bite, and release rodents in less than a half second, allowing the stricken animal to run off harmlessly and die. Then the snake must follow the prey's chemical trail to find and consume the meal. In addition to their primary adult diet of kangaroo rats and other rodents, Mohave rattlesnakes of all ages also eat lizards. Interestingly, the snakes tend to strike and hold lizards rather than releasing them, apparently knowing that lizards pose little threat of injury to the rattlesnake.

Fascinating research into just how Mohave rattlesnakes and sidewinders ambush kangaroo rats has been carried out in recent years by Rulon Clark and his students at San Diego State University, recently in collaboration with Tim Higham's lab at the Riverside campus of the University of California. Using high-speed night-vision cameras, these scientists have been able to document many rattlesnake/kangaroo rat encounters in great detail. While the rattlesnakes kill and eat lots of kangaroo rats, Rulon and his colleagues have discovered that the kangaroo rats are frequently able to avoid the rattlesnakes' strikes – particularly if they have already detected the rattlesnake or are in "high alert" mode because of another recent rattlesnake encounter. The rats' lightning-quick twisting leaps to avoid strikes, sometimes combined with kicking the rattlesnakes away in mid-air, earned them the nickname "ninja rats" among the researchers. You can watch some of these amazing videos at www.ninjarat.org.

Newborn Mohave rattlesnakes are the size of a pencil, weigh less than an ounce, and are too small to eat even an adult mouse, so they prey heavily on lizards. Probably not coincidentally, baby rattlesnakes are born at the same time that lizard eggs are hatching, providing a good supply of bite-sized prey at just the right time for the young rattlesnakes.

WATER AND HYDRATION

Like most small predators in arid environments, Mohave rattlesnakes get almost all of their water from the body water of their prey (Nagy, 1987). Summer conditions are hot and bone dry in most places where Mohave rattlesnakes live and surface water is rarely available. Mohaves will certainly drink when they can and will even drink rainwater they trap between their coils during storms (Cardwell, 2006). But all terrestrial animals are about 70% liquid water, so a four-ounce rodent contains almost three ounces of water plus an ounce or so of protein. As a result, these small desert predators thrive in

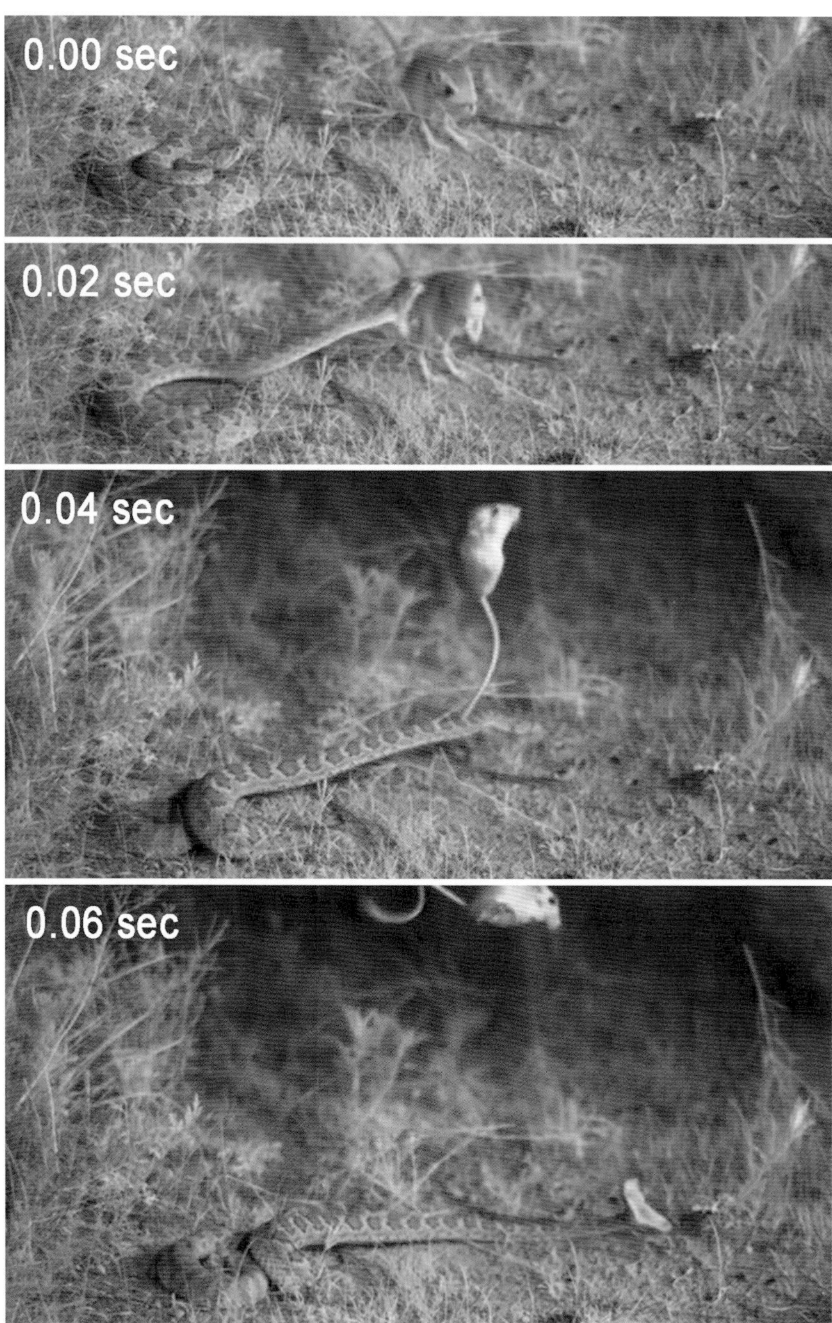

Frame grabs from high-speed night-vision video of a wild Mohave rattlesnake striking at a kangaroo rat and the rodent's remarkable ability to avoid the strike. Video courtesy San Diego State University and University of California Riverside; See www.ninjarat.org for this and other videos.

extraordinarily dry conditions with a low metabolic rate, eating frequently, and minimizing evaporative water loss by avoiding excessive sun, wind, heat and exposed skin area when necessary.

BODY TEMPERATURE AND THERMAL TOLERANCE

Rattlesnakes tolerate being cold much better than getting too hot. So long as their tissues do not freeze, they can warm up and be fine (Klauber, 1972). But if they get too hot, the proteins in their brains begin to denature (protein molecules unfold and come apart), quickly killing the snakes. This lethal body temperature is somewhere close to 100°F. Using surgically-implanted temperature-sensing radio transmitters in my field study, I recorded very few body temperatures above 92°F and the highest body temperature I recorded in living (and surviving) wild Mohave rattlesnakes was 97°F, recorded only three times out of thousands of body temperatures.

The lowest body temperature I have documented was 47°F, recorded on five occasions during winter hibernation. Of 3,522 recorded observations that included body temperatures over 40 consecutive months, the median 95% ranged from 50°F to 91°F.

Demonstrating that the potential for rattlesnake encounters cannot be discounted in cool weather, I found multiple Mohave rattlesnakes engaged in all sorts of behavior with body temperatures below 60°F. Some of the coldest examples were several animals in ambush coils (apparently hunting) with body temperatures of 49–50°F, a 59° animal swallowing a ground squirrel, an animal drinking rain water off its own skin at 52°, and a copulating pair at 55° (male's body temperature; the female had no transmitter).

SEASONAL MOVEMENT

Adult female Mohave rattlesnakes move much less than adult males, with average daily movement of females being about one third that of males (Cardwell, 2008). Put simply, you find females where there are resources and you find males where there are females. The females tend to stay where there is ample food, winter shelter, and where they have a place to maintain just the right temperature during pregnancy. Then the males search for them during the courtship season. As a result, average daily movement for males at my California study site sometimes approached 300 feet per day during the breeding season, while females averaged 100 feet or less. It is not surprising, then, that male home ranges were about 5½ times larger than those of females, averaging about 78 acres for males – equivalent to almost 60 NFL football

A Mohave rattlesnake drinking rain water it traps between flattened coils during a summer thunderstorm.

fields, compared to about 13 acres or 10 football fields for females (Cardwell, 2008).

I should note that average daily movement of both sexes, as well as reproductive behavior, was greatly reduced at my California study site during the severe drought of 2002. I believe that reduced movement and courtship during the drought was a consequence of the need to minimize evaporative water loss by remaining coiled, thereby protecting much of the snakes' skin surface from the dry air while ambush-hunting for prey and the water contained in that prey (Cardwell, 2013).

During more typical weather, however, females tend to spend almost all their time hunting for food, unless they are pregnant and remaining inactive while "thermoregulating" for two months or more before giving birth. Males, on the other hand, spend much of their life searching for females. As a result, they spend less time hunting for food between spring emergence and the end of the spring courtship in mid or late May. Mid-summer is spent seeking daytime shelter from the heat and hunting for rodents – primarily kangaroo rats and other nocturnal species – at night. By the end of August, reproductive hormones return and finding females begins to compete with finding food

This Mohave rattlesnake is swallowing a large round-tailed ground squirrel (*Xerospermophilus tereticaudus*) at dusk. This strictly-diurnal rodent was undoubtedly struck earlier in the day, a testament to the time often required to locate a meal after the typical strike-and-release attack of the rattlesnake.

again. This cycle is aided in the Sonoran Desert where the monsoon season of late summer brings cloudy skies and frequent warm rain, producing a flurry of growth and activity in all organisms, including rattlesnakes.

Mohave rattlesnakes are neither strictly diurnal nor nocturnal. Rather, they are active when surface temperatures are not too extreme. When it is too hot or too cold on the surface, Mohave rattlesnakes take refuge underground, usually in burrows previously excavated by animals like kangaroo rats, ground squirrels, tortoises and kit foxes. Otherwise, we find Mohaves hunting for food and mates during the day in spring and fall when evenings are cold and daytime temperatures are moderate but they gradually switch to more nocturnal activity during summer, when the evenings are warm and daytime surface temperatures become deadly. The bottom line is this: if you are comfortable in shirt sleeves, Mohave rattlesnakes are likely to be active no matter the time of day or night – but you cannot discount the possibility of a rattlesnake encounter in very cool weather.

PREDATION

Few credible reports exist of predation specifically on Mohave rattlesnakes, although they are almost certainly susceptible to the same predators as other rattlesnakes of similar size in similar habitat, with babies being eaten by a larger set of predators than adults. Because we do not yet have the technology to radio-track very small rattlesnakes for very long, we can only hypothesize about why we see so few young-of-the-year in the spring, even though they were plentiful a few months before in the fall. It is apparent that few survive to adulthood and I believe predation is the major cause of this mortality. Roadrunners (*Geococcyx californianus*) and common kingsnakes (*Lampropeltis* sp.) are well known rattlesnake predators but birds like red-tailed hawks (*Buteo jamaicensis*) and snakes like coachwhips (*Masticophis flagellum*) eat rattlesnakes, too, especially very small ones. Badgers (*Taxidea taxus*) and coyotes (*Canis latrans*) regularly eat rattlesnakes, including adults, which they are able to dig out of rodent burrows (Klauber, 1972). Although burrowing owls (*Athene cunicularia*) may eat very young rattlesnakes, I found one of my telemetered adult male Mohave rattlesnakes sharing an abandoned kit fox (*Vulpes microtis*) burrow with at least one burrowing owl during two consecutive winters (Cardwell, 2005).

Kit foxes were common on my California study site and often followed me during my nocturnal forays to collect data from telemetered rattlesnakes. These bold little canids are very curious and often sat a few meters away watching me collect data at each rattlesnake. I wondered for a while if I was leading

Rare images of a wild coyote preying on a large rattlesnake. Although this snake is a different species, Mohaves are clearly on the coyote menu. Photos courtesy of Alan Schmierer.

them to their dinner, especially after a couple of my telemetered rattlesnakes disappeared, leaving only chewed transmitters in the dirt. Then on one lucky night, I witnessed an encounter between an adult female Mohave rattlesnake and a kit fox. The snake was rattling furiously in full defensive display with the adult fox five feet or so away. I stayed back and watched as the fox stretched its neck and nose as far as it could toward the rattlesnake – just out of strike range, sniffing the air. Then it retreated a few feet, trotted around the snake, and approached again from the other side. As the fox circled, the rattlesnake pivoted too, always facing the fox and rattling vigorously. The whole encounter lasted only a minute or so before the fox turned and trotted into the darkness. Klauber (1972) relates some inconclusive evidence that gray foxes (*Urocyon cinereoargenteus*) "may sometimes kill rattlers" but he makes no mention of kit foxes as rattlesnake predators. Kit foxes weigh less than half as much as gray foxes and, while they may well kill and eat juvenile rattlesnakes, I am convinced that they are not significant predators of adults. However, coyotes

Bobcats are also predators of adult rattlesnakes. Here a bobcat is caught preying on a western diamondback. Images courtesy of Laura Lucky.

Sonoran Desert Scrub habitat west of Tucson, Arizona, where Mohave rattlesnakes share the landscape with western diamondbacks and sidewinders.

were always present at my study site, although they were much shyer than the kit foxes, and coyotes are well known to prey on adult rattlesnakes (Klauber, 1972).

While I can find nothing published in the scientific literature about rattlesnake predation by bobcats, a real estate agent recorded a bobcat killing a 2½-foot western diamondback on a suburban Scottsdale street in April 2018. The confrontation, televised by KNXV Phoenix, had obviously been going on for some time when recording started and the rattlesnake was already tired and injured. The bobcat repeatedly slapped with its paws and bit the snake while dodging strikes before finally grabbing the snake by the head and trotting off. There was no word about what effect the incident had on the house-hunting clients in the agent's car!

Mohave Rattlesnake Bite and its Effects

9

PREDATORY VS.DEFENSIVE BITES

Rattlesnakes bite for two reasons: to kill something to eat and to defend themselves. With the exception of bites by long-term captive rattlesnakes, people are bitten defensively. Wild rattlesnakes do not mistake us for food. And while it has been well established that rattlesnakes inject more venom into larger prey and vice versa during predatory bites (Herbert and Hayes, 2008), it has also been shown that the amount of venom delivered during defensive bites is much more variable, including a significant percentage of "dry bites" – bites with little or no venom injected (Russell, 1980). In other words, rattlesnakes kill something to eat regularly and get very good at it but the same does not apply to defensive bites.

In fact, in my decades of experience interacting with countless rattlesnakes, including many Mohaves, I have come to view defensive strikes as a panic response by a frightened animal, usually only after hiding, fleeing and intimidating have failed. And I believe that many – if not most – rattlesnakes may go their entire lives without having to bite anything defensively. As a result, a rattlesnake bite to a person is likely inflicted by a panicked animal employing a last-resort action it has never tried before, making the results (i.e., how much venom was injected) highly unpredictable.

CLINICAL EFFECTS: SIGNS AND SYMPTOMS OF ENVENOMATION

Mohave rattlesnakes are well known to produce two very different types of venoms (Chapter 5) and human deaths are extraordinarily rare. And while the venom type (neurotoxic or tissue-destroying) may be generally inferred by where the snake was encountered, the borders between neurotoxic venom-A and tissue-destroying venom-B populations are not well defined and a few individuals produce both types of toxin in the same venom.

In any case, there is no way to determine how much or which type of venom has been injected immediately after a Mohave rattlesnake bite. Despite the claims by some about painful rattlesnake bites, there is usually little initial sensation. The bite is very quick, the fangs are small and very sharp, and it happens by surprise. The bitten person feels the contact but there is little or no

Plains and Great Basin Grassland habitat at 4,500 feet elevation in Chino Valley, Yavapai County, Arizona, where a fatal Mohave rattlesnake bite occurred in 2007.

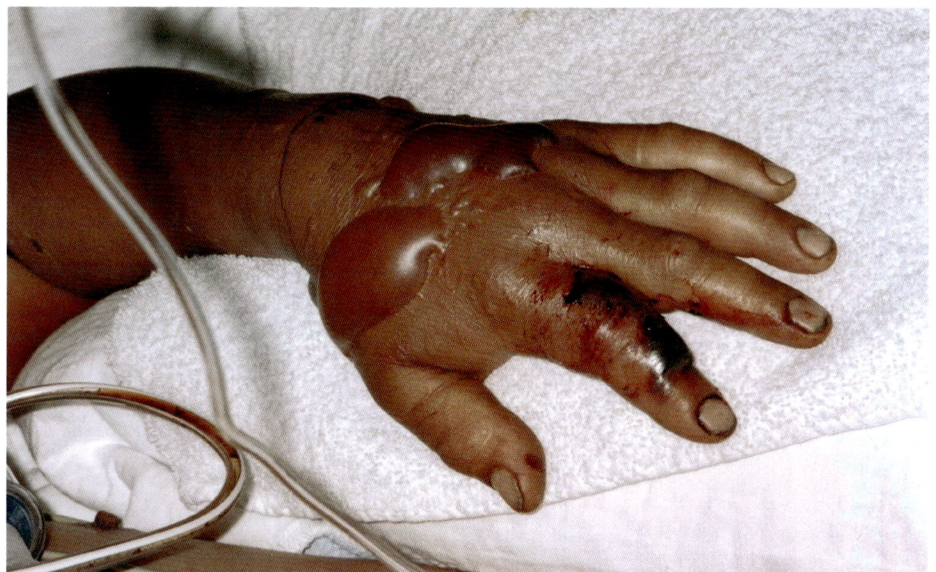

Effects of a rattlesnake bite full of tissue-destroying metalloprotease. Photo courtesy of Sean Bush.

immediate discomfort. The first reaction is usually disbelief: "Wow! Did that just happen?" (Of course, a stronger expletive is likely used!) It is only a few seconds later when a couple of tiny droplets of blood appear that it becomes apparent that, yes, you've just been bitten by a rattlesnake! I know; I've been bitten twice.

There are exceptions, cases where the snake hangs on or where the fangs or other teeth get tangled in clothing. Such cases do occur but are not common. The bite is usually over almost instantly with no initial effect. So what should you expect to happen next?

Rattlesnake fangs are not terribly long; it takes a large rattlesnake to have ¼-inch fangs. As a result, the venom is usually deposited in the skin or in the fatty layer just below it. While there are many potential variables, probably the two most important are which type of venom is involved and how much was injected. Neither question has a quick answer.

It is important to note that the other variables contributing to the unpredictability of the effects of a rattlesnake bite are numerous, including the size, age and health of the victim, as well as previous exposure to rattlesnake venom and antivenom. The effects of venom-A and venom-B bites are not always distinct regardless of where the snake was encountered and a mixture of signs and symptoms should not be surprising.

BITES BY VENOM-B MOHAVE RATTLESNAKES

Bites by venom-B Mohaves result in injuries that are similar to the bites of many other rattlesnakes, such as the western diamondback. The tissue-destroying toxins begin their work immediately, destroying cell membranes around the bite as the venom spreads into the lymphatic system under the skin. Early symptoms include swelling and throbbing pain that often begins within minutes and gradually progresses away from the fang punctures. How soon these symptoms begin and how quickly they progress is likely related to how much venom was injected but other factors are involved, too.

Over time (minutes to hours, depending primarily on how much venom and how deeply it was deposited), swelling of the bitten area can become severe, bruising occurs as venom reaches and destroys capillaries, and large blisters filled with either clear fluid or blood known as "bullae" can form on the skin surface.

Total tissue destruction may occur surrounding the bite site where the venom is most concentrated. Known as "necrosis" (tissue death), the tissue turns from badly bruised to black and shrinks into a hard mass as other effects subside over time. This dead mass will eventually slough off, sometimes requiring surgical removal (debridement), leaving a permanent scar. In serious bites, such scars can be very large and missing tissue can involve not just skin and muscle but also tendons, ligaments, and nerves – sometimes resulting in permanent deformity, loss of range of motion of joints and even amputations of fingers, etc.

There are other potentially dangerous systemic problems that can occur with serious venom-B bites, including coagulation abnormalities resulting in spontaneous bleeding in and around the body as well as acute kidney failure due to "rhabdomyolysis," where the kidneys are overwhelmed and clogged as they try to filter out cellular debris that accumulates in the blood from skeletal muscle destruction. Widespread inflammation, sometimes compounded by spontaneous bleeding remote from the bite site, can reduce fluid volume, leading to compromised circulation, lowered blood pressure (hypotension) and shock.

If these injuries sound frightening, they are – or certainly can be. But they can be prevented by avoiding being bitten (Chapter 13) or minimized by prompt and proper medical treatment (Chapter 14).

BITES BY VENOM-A MOHAVE RATTLESNAKES

Venom-A Mohaves, characterized by the presence of Mojave toxin and the absence of tissue-destroying metalloproteinase in their venom, typically

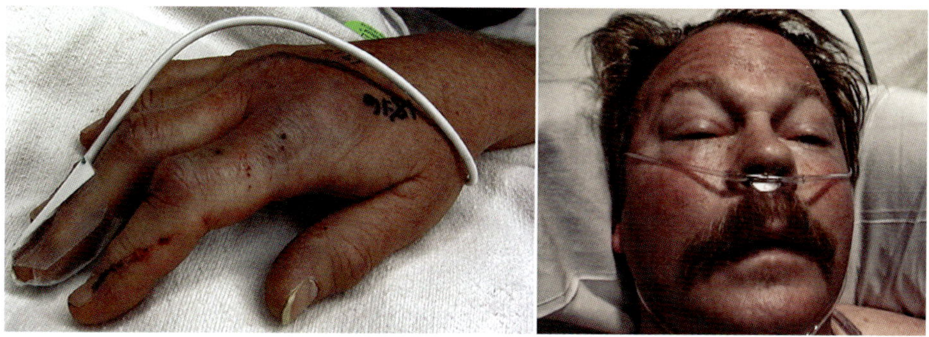

A venom-A Mohave rattlesnake bite. Note the lack of local effects around the bite on the index finger and the patient's drooping eyelids (ptosis). Photos courtesy of Sean Bush with patient consent.

produce little or no effects around the bite site. There is sometimes no swelling, bruising, pain or any of the other local problems usually associated with venom-B bites. This may cause physicians to underestimate the seriousness of the envenomation, as a serious venom-A bite can look like a dry bite for several hours.

But Mojave toxin is a potent "pre-synaptic" neurotoxin, the effects of which are systemic. The result is that onset of symptoms is usually delayed because the venom must be absorbed into the lymphatic system at the bite site, which slowly drains the venom into the blood where it is eventually spread all around the body.

The first noticeable symptom produced by Mojave toxin is usually ptosis, or difficulty keeping the eyelids open. This may be followed or accompanied by fatigue, low blood pressure (hypotension), slurred speech (dysarthria) and difficulty swallowing (dysphagia). Over time, as more Mojave toxin finds and disrupts nerve synapses, symptoms can progress to involve paralysis of the diaphragm with resulting respiratory difficulty, which can eventually be fatal. It must be kept in mind, however, that the effects of any bite may be different in different people. Not only are the rattlesnakes and their venoms variable, but the size, health and physiology of the bitten person can have a profound effect on the illness produced by a rattlesnake bite.

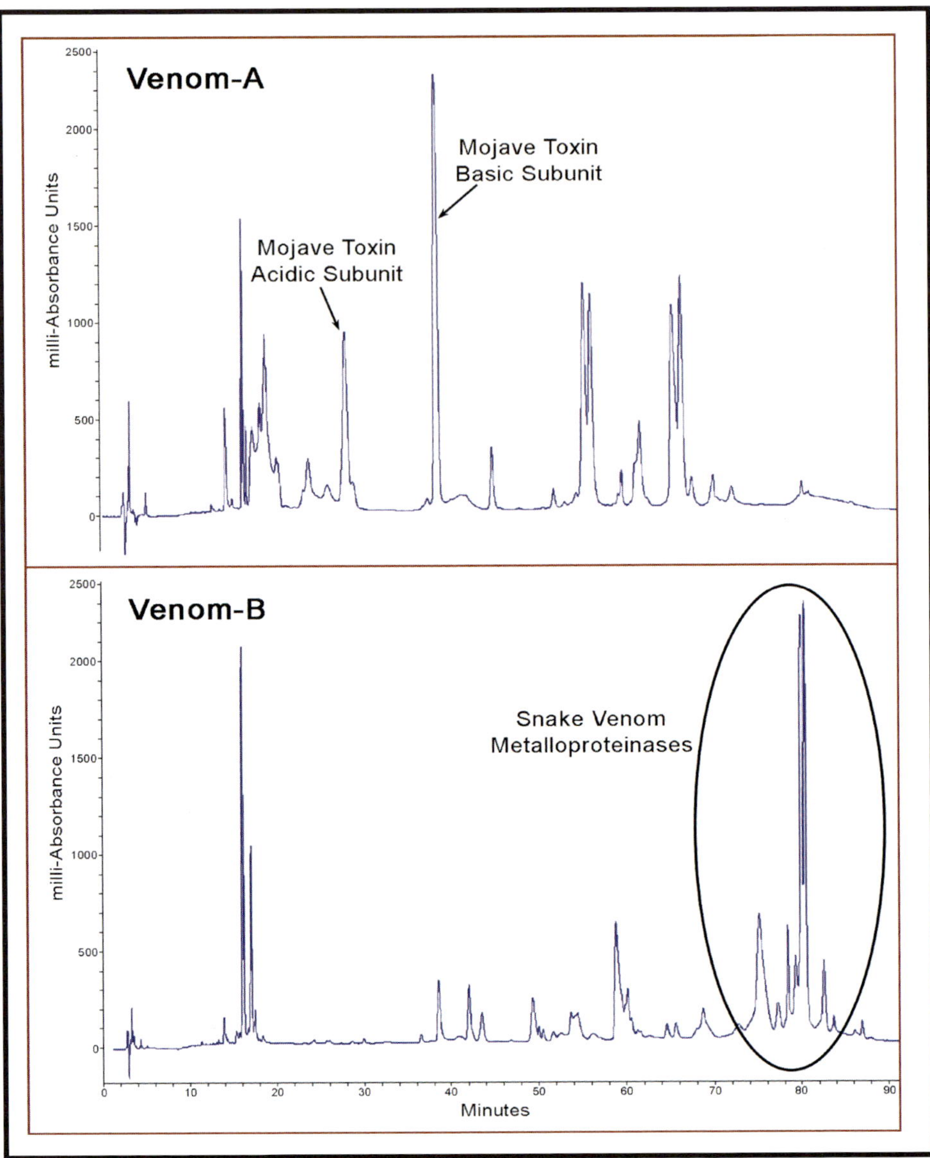

Chromatography is a standard technique used to separate and identify molecules in a liquid; each peak is a different molecule and height indicates abundance. These chromatograms are characteristic of neurotoxic Mohave rattlesnake venom-A (top) and tissue-destroying venom-B (bottom). Mohave toxin is composed of two distinct molecules while metalloproteinases are actually a family of similar toxins. Adapted from Zancolli et al., 2016.

Mohave Rattlesnake Myths and the News Media 10

I was once expressing my frustration about rattlesnake myths to a good friend who is also a world-renowned arachnologist (spider expert) and he asked me this:

> "If the two of us were at a party and you were in one corner telling people that rattlesnakes are shy creatures that want nothing to do with people… while I was in another corner describing how I had been chased up a tree by a rattlesnake, who do you think would have the larger crowd?"

Sadly, he made a good point.

We have all seen how editors use sensational headlines about bad news to grab our attention and get us to click on the story, pick up the newspaper, or leave the channel unchanged. I'm not blaming the editors personally, since I'm sure they have lots of data to show that those kinds of headlines are most effective to attract an audience. But combine that with the general public's near-universal fear of snakes and people in positions of authority repeating sensational rumors, and it is suddenly easier to understand how the news media breathes life into so many false claims.

For example, a September 1995 article in a small California newspaper was titled "New Type of Snake Jeopardizes Baby After Bite." In an interview with the California father about his critically-ill son hospitalized in Arizona, the reporter states that the two-year-old boy was bitten "by a snake that experts in Arizona say is a spine-chilling combination of the Coontail Rattlesnake and the deadly Mojave Green Rattlesnake." A few lines later, the article states "Authorities informed [the father] that the new breed of rattlesnake is far more deadly than either of the species from which it is derived." Then quoting the father directly, it said, "They also told me that the only way for these two snakes to breed is in captivity. It looks as though somebody is doing this on purpose." Quoting further from the father, "Apparently they have just shown up in the last year or so," followed by "I was told that it is at least three times more toxic than a bite from an ordinary Mojave Green." (The Apple Valley News, September 1, 1995:2 and 7)

These assertions, attributed to "experts" and "authorities" in Arizona, would be laughable if it were not for a critically-injured child and a terrified and badly misinformed father. The "coontail" rattlesnake referred to in the article is almost certainly the western damondback with its black and white-ringed tail – the most commonly encountered rattlesnake in Arizona and certainly capable of delivering a life-threatening bite, especially to a small child. But there is zero evidence that there is (or was) a recent population of Mohave x western diamondback hybrids, despite intense interest in wild hybrid rattlesnakes by numerous well-qualified scientists (see Chapter 6). The only part of the story that is more shameful than the recent hybrid claim is the suggestion that someone is artificially producing a free-ranging population of such snakes. If anyone had bothered to make a call to any one of Arizona's many actual rattlesnake experts located at various universities, zoos, and at the Arizona Poison and Drug Information Center, they would have learned that the entire recent deadly hybrid idea is an urban legend with no basis in fact.

In another case, a flurry of stories appeared in multiple southern California print and broadcast news outlets in July 2012 about a child bitten by a Mohave rattlesnake in coastal Orange County, California. According to news reports, "doctors recognized the symptoms as a bite from the especially toxic rattlesnake, the Mojave Green" (CBS News, July 10, 2012, 6PM). Despite the fact that the closest Mohave rattlesnake population was 100 miles away on the other side of a mountain range, it is likely that doctors observed signs and symptoms of neurotoxicity and ignored well-documented evidence of neurotoxicity following bites by the locally common southern Pacific rattlesnake (*Crotalus oreganus helleri*).

I believe most people accept as fact such pronouncements by well-respected people in positions of authority – like emergency medicine physicians. And I am equally sure that this case erroneously established the local existence of Mohave greens in the minds of a huge number of citizens far from where Mohaves actually exist. As a result, the urban legend status of Mohave greens was greatly enhanced.

Such errors could easily be avoided if the physicians and/or journalists involved had made the effort to consult with a qualified herpetologist. In fact, most regional poison control centers now have on-call herpetologists available to identify cell phone photographs and answer other questions. Why did these folks not reach out for advice? Because I'm sure they thought they knew… neurotoxicity must indicate a Mohave green!

As I mentioned in the Preface, I was initially intimidated during my first few rattlesnake talks at medical conferences but soon found that a lot of medical professionals hold the same misguided beliefs and have the same questions as

▶WILDLIFE

'Tis the season to be wary: Mojave Green rattlesnakes now hatching, expert warns

According to exp
snake in question is f
ly in Arizona bec
Coontail Rattles
restricted to that envi
"Apparently they hav
shown up in the last yea
so," said "They
that olive green color o
Mojave Green, but they
have the Coontail ring pa
on their tail." said
the combination of the nerve-destroying toxin of the Mojave Green with the tissue-destroying poison of the Coontail combine to produce a greatly increased threat to the bite victim. "I was told that it is at least three times more toxic than a bite from an ordinary Mojave Green."

Toxins from these snakebites can lie dormant in a person's system for years and can be unexpectedly reactivated by trauma.

Unlike adult snakes, baby rattlers have no sense of how much venom to inject into their victims, said Dr. ... So, although the venom of babies is no more lethal than an adult, its bite could inject more poison.

Authorities
that the new breed of rattlesnake is far more deadly than
either of the species from which
it is derived... "They said that
there was

Not only are the Mojave greens aggressive, but their venom is both a hemotoxin (affect-
ng red blood cells that carry
xygen to tissue) and neurotoxin
destroying nerves and nervous
ssues). If a bite victim is not treated within 20 minutes, permanent damage can occur.

"Right now, this snake is considered the most poisonous, dangerous snake in North America," said.

The Mojave green can reach lengths of seven feet with babies ranging from 6- to-8 inches. The babies are more dangerous because they haven't yet learned to how to conserve their venom. Of-

The dreaded and lethal Mojave Green rattlesnakes have

other people. I have been told by many physicians that snakebite is not a topic covered in medical school and most physicians never see a rattlesnake bite in their careers. The exceptions are, of course, emergency room physicians at hospitals in areas where snakebites occur frequently or at regional trauma centers that receive patients transferred from multiple suburban hospitals.

So here are the most common myths concerning Mohave rattlesnakes and Mohave greens. Later, in Chapter 12, I will cover other general rattlesnake myths, most or all of which are also applied to Mohave rattlesnakes.

MYTH #1 – MOHAVE GREENS ARE SOME KIND OF UNUSUAL ANIMAL

False! Mohave green is the name given to a mythical creature that has grown out of the many false claims about Mohave rattlesnakes. Just like other animals, different rattlesnake species are identified and named based on subtle differences between them and Mohave rattlesnakes are simply one of many rattlesnake species that have been evolving for millions of years. Mohaves, in particular, have been described and studied by people for more than 150 years.

MYTH #2 – MOHAVE RATTLESNAKES ARE PARTICULARLY AGGRESSIVE

False! For many years, I didn't know what to say when people would speak up at my public presentations, claiming that Mohave rattlesnakes had attacked or chased them. Wanting to avoid arguing with them in front of an audience, I would point out that a furiously rattling and striking rattlesnake is behaving defensively, not aggressively as we might expect from a bear or large shark.

But what do you say to someone who insists that a Mohave rattlesnake chased his family into their car and bit at the tires as they drove away? (A story actually related to me a couple years ago!) My answer now is simple: I pull out my cell phone, hold it up, and remind everyone that we all now carry a video camera in our pocket. And we all have the opportunity to post the first video of an attacking Mohave rattlesnake on YouTube! If rattlesnakes were chasing people, YouTube would be full of the videos.

The famous 20th century herpetologist Clifford Pope once characterized rattlesnakes as "first cowards, then bluffers, and last of all warriors" (Pope, 1937). In my experience, that accurately characterizes rattlesnake behavior, including Mohaves. When a rattlesnake encounters another animal, it has evolved to quickly evaluate three issues: Can it eat me? Can I eat it? Can I mate with it?

The mistaken belief that Mohave rattlesnakes are particularly dangerous compared to other rattlesnake species is deeply embedded in the folklore of the American Southwest, as evidenced by this old sign discovered in Clark County, Nevada. Photo courtesy of Louis W. Porras.

The bottom line is this: neither I nor any of my herpetologist colleagues have ever had a rattlesnake attack us – including Mohaves, despite many thousands of very close encounters. However, as I hinted above, when rattlesnakes are surprised, approached too closely, and especially if stepped on, they often respond explosively – rattling, striking (not always in that order) and trying to look as intimidating and dangerous as possible. But if you leave them alone, they will leave you alone. See Chapter 13 for more details.

My Only Snake "Attack"

In my many thousands of snake encounters over half a century, I have had only one snake "attack" me, and by that I mean advance toward me with the intention of biting me – which it did! But I provoked it and deserved the bite. The animal was a large red coachwhip (*Masticophis flagellum*), which is a common, non-venomous, diurnal desert snake that is well known for being alert, fast, and quick to flee when approached – making them difficult to photograph or catch. One hot morning, I came across a four-foot coachwhip in an area without nearby rodent burrows into which it could retreat. In an effort to finally get some decent photos of the species, I ran to head it off each time it tried to flee. With no holes available, it eventually took shelter in the dappled shade of a creosote bush. After several photos and heading off several more attempts to flee, the snake finally had apparently had enough. It suddenly charged straight at me with its mouth open and bit my pant leg! Astonished and now feeling bad for having tormented the poor animal, I allowed it to finally make its escape. Although it clearly advanced on me with the intention of biting, the behavior was also obviously a last resort defensive tactic. So, despite my tongue-in-cheek claim of having been "attacked" in this case, the fact remains that our native snakes (venomous and harmless) only confront people in self-defense, after hiding and flight have proven ineffective.

MYTH #3 – MOHAVE RATTLESNAKES ARE PARTICULARLY DEADLY

False! As explained in Chapter 5, Mohaves rate very high in lethality tests carried out with lab mice but those results do not translate to people. Mohave rattlesnakes are common animals and responsible for many snakebites every year in the United States, yet there are only about five or six annual snakebite deaths. And most of those fatalities happen in places where there are no Mohave rattlesnakes. Check out the references provided in Chapter 5.

MYTH #4 – ANTIVENOM DOESN'T WORK AGAINST MOHAVE BITES

False! We currently have two FDA-approved rattlesnake antivenoms available in the United States and both work well against Mohave rattlesnakes with either venom type (neurotoxic venom-A or tissue-destroying venom-B). CroFab® has been available since 2000 and contains antibodies raised against the venoms of four pitvipers, one of which is Mohave rattlesnake venom-A. Then Anavip® became available in 2018, containing antibodies raised against two pitvipers, including the neotropical rattlesnake, *Crotalus durissus*. Neotropical rattlesnake venom contains Crotoxin, another presynaptic neurotoxin nearly identical in molecular structure to Mojave toxin, making Anavip® quite effective in treating bites by venom-A Mohaves.

The antibodies in both CroFab® and Anavip® that are raised against the venoms of other species in their respective blends make both products effective against the more common tissue-destroying venoms of other rattlesnakes, including venom-B Mohaves. Much more information about antivenoms can be found in Chapter 14.

MYTH #5 – MOHAVE RATTLESNAKE VENOM LIES DORMANT IN THE BODY, ONLY TO CAUSE PROBLEMS LATER IN LIFE.

False! Just like other foreign proteins, Mohave rattlesnake venom is attacked and neutralized by our immune systems – and treatment with antivenom gives that process a very vital assist. While rattlesnake bites can cause life-long problems, such problems are the result of damage done to various tissues in the hours and days following the bite, not by active venom lingering in the body for months or years.

MYTH #6 – MOHAVE RATTLESNAKES HAVE A MYSTERIOUS ORIGIN

False! There is now ample irrefutable genetic evidence that Mohave rattlesnakes evolved from a common ancestor shared with other rattlesnakes more than 3 million years ago. The mysterious origin myth is believed to have started with the fact that no one could find the original museum specimen used to describe the species – until 2013 – due to a specimen tagging error at the Smithsonian Institution between 1861 and 1882, followed by a publication error in 1900. In fact, the original "holotype" specimen has been sitting in a jar of alcohol at the Academy of Natural Sciences of Philadelphia for over 150 years. See Chapter 4 for more details.

MYTH #7 – MOHAVE RATTLESNAKES PRODUCE 75 TO 125 BABIES PER YEAR AND ARE RAPIDLY DISPLACING OTHER DESERT SNAKES

False! Similar to other medium-sized rattlesnakes, the average litter size for Mohaves is eight, females cannot produce more than one litter per year, and they usually skip years between broods. Females usually drop 30-50% of their body weight when they give birth and, because food and water is relatively scarce in the desert, it often takes more than one season to replenish enough body fat to sustain another pregnancy. Mohave rattlesnakes are common snakes in many areas but there is no evidence that their numbers are not stable, as are the numbers of most other desert snakes in undeveloped areas.

These hoax "Mohave green" den photos went viral in 2008.

11 Internet Hysteria

The Internet has facilitated the circulation of all sorts of information about Mohave rattlesnakes, most of which is exaggerated or downright false. Interestingly, when outrageous online claims are politely countered with accurate information by more rational people, the result is too often either silence from the original source or occasionally a profanity-laced tirade defending the original misleading post.

Misleading posts sometimes involve misidentified photos of rattlesnakes. Over the years, I have seen a handful of photos labeled "Mojave gold" and "Mohave red" rattlesnakes. One was even accompanied with the notation that the "Mojave red" is not quite as aggressive as the "Mojave green." Reported locations for these photos were the desert of northeastern San Bernardino and southeastern Inyo Counties in California. Each of these snakes were unmistakably either Panamint rattlesnakes (*Crotalus stephensi*; formerly *Crotalus mitchellii stephensi*) or southwestern speckled rattlesnakes (*Crotalus pyrrhus*; formerly *Crotalus mitchellii pyrrhus*). There is even a beer called "Mohave gold" with a caricature of a rattlesnake on the label, produced by a local brewery not far away.

However, the best example of Internet hysteria is a series of five photos that began circulating as email attachments in the spring of 2008, showing dozens of olive green rattlesnakes piled on top of one another on a sparsely vegetated hillside – obviously a spring or fall gathering at a hibernation den. The first of many emails forwarded to me containing the photos originated from a high ranking officer at Edwards Air Force Base in California and was titled, "Mojave Green Snakes are Out!" The email had been distributed widely around the sprawling Mohave Desert base and warned folks to "Be careful in the desert--this is crazy--watch out." After warning not to let kids or pets wander off of established paths because "these guys are much more aggressive" than western diamondbacks, the original email states, "When you go out in the desert you enter the food chain and you AREN'T at the top. These guys are WAY above us in the pecking order…"

Well, two things were immediately obvious: First, Mohave rattlesnakes are not known to den communally; they spend the winter by themselves in rodent burrows. Second and most important, the snakes in the photos were not even Mohave rattlesnakes. Instead, they looked like prairie rattlesnakes (*Crotalus*

Found in AZ
Sent by: Aug 08/18/13 11:03 AM

Happy golfing everyone!

This is why you shouldn't go looking for the golf balls hit 'Out of Bounds' in Arizona !!!

Better add the .410 to the golf bag.

Of course, there is no St. Johns County in Arizona. This photo has been making the online rounds since 2009 with various captions, some claiming it shows "a 15 foot western diamondback…found near the St. Augustine outlet, in a new KB homes subdivision just south of Mesa Az." Shooting the photo with the snake close to the camera and the people a few feet away makes the snake look huge. In fact, the photo was pirated from the September 30, 2009, edition of the Saint Augustine Record in St. Johns County, Florida. The snake is a good size eastern diamondback rattlesnake, the largest rattlesnake species with a maximum length of only around 8 feet. Note the twisting body indicating that the poor animal is still alive. The original photo attribution read "Contributed photos"

viridis), which are well known to gather together for the winter but they are not native to California – not even close.

Over several months, people forwarded emails to me with the same five photos attached that had originated from all over the western United States. I exchanged emails with people who claimed to have taken the photos in several California locations, as well as in places like Flagstaff, Arizona; Riverton, Utah; Amarillo, Texas; and Richland, Washington. Some of these emails had been disseminated by a large law enforcement agency and even by a public health official, all claiming that the snakes were Mohave greens. In several cases, local news media had picked up the erroneous story and spread it further.

I eventually back-tracked an email chain to the actual photographers, who were quite surprised that their photos had been so widely circulated and caused such a stir. It turned out that two families on a 2008 Mother's Day outing in Fremont County, Wyoming, came across the emerging den of prairie rattlesnakes and several people took pictures. Multiple people from both families have confirmed the story and the actual photographer sent me the original five digital files. Examination of the metadata imbedded in the photos corroborated his claim of time and place. The photos are reproduced here with the photographer's consent.

The five photos were innocently emailed to friends who forwarded them to others and, well, you can imagine the rest. Within a couple of weeks, they were a den of Mohave greens terrorizing the entire western United States! They are still being circulated, although much less frequently.

Chihuahuan Desert Scrub habitat in the "Cochise Filter" at about 4,500 feet elevation straddling the southern portion of the Arizona-New Mexico state line, which also separates the Mohave-Sonoran clade from the Chihuahuan clade of Mohave rattlesnakes..

Other Rattlesnake Myths 12

MYTH #1 – BABY RATTLESNAKES ARE MORE DANGEROUS THAN ADULTS

False! This is, by far, the most common rattlesnake myth. When I ask audiences about who has heard this one, nearly everyone raises their hand. The reason most frequently given is that baby rattlesnakes have not yet learned how to meter their venom.

The fact is that baby rattlesnakes are just miniatures of the adults in every way, including the size of the glands that produce and store venom. I like to use the example of venom yields from an adult male Mohave compared to a two-month-old baby (next page). The baby weighs in at just over ½ ounce, while the adult weights very close to a pound – more than 24 times larger by weight than the baby. The photos show the actual venom I extracted from these rattlesnakes: yellow venom pooled in the bottom of the beaker from the adult while the baby produced a single drop that ran halfway down the glass.

While this illustrates my point visually, it represents only one venom extraction. But venom yield data collected by multiple researchers and summarized by Jim Glenn and Richard Straight (1982) is far more compelling. According to values calculated from hundreds of extractions, the average venom yield (dry weight) from juvenile (about 12-inch) rattlesnakes is about 1–2 milligrams, while the average yield from 1-meter (39-inch) adults is about 160 milligrams – about 100X the yield of the babies (Glenn and Straight, 1982:66–67).

And we have clinical evidence to bust this myth, as well. After many years without good data on snake size versus snakebite severity published in a scholarly peer-reviewed journal (although see helpful comments by Drs. Willis Wingert and Linda Chan, 1988), Drs. Donald Janes, Sean Bush, and Gita Kolluru analyzed 145 rattlesnake bites treated in southern California between 1995 and 2004 and published their findings in 2010. These data were collected by Sean Bush, an emergency department physician at Loma Linda University Medical Center, sixty miles east of Los Angeles. LLUMC is a Level 1 regional trauma center that sees up to 60,000 emergency room patients a year, including dozens of rattlesnake bites from throughout San Bernardino and Riverside counties, as well as portions of several others.

Typical venom extractions from an adult male Mohave rattlesnake weighing nearly a pound (left) and from a juvenile male weighing just over ½ ounce (right). Even if babies don't "control" their venom, they have only a tiny fraction of the venom available in an adult's much larger venom glands.

As part of his routine medical record, Dr. Bush documented the size of the biting snake based on estimates by the patient and witnesses, the distance between fang punctures, and occasionally by examination of the snake itself. (Yes, people now and then bring rattlesnakes into the hospital, often dead but sometimes not!) The analysis divided the biting rattlesnakes into three general size categories: less than 16 inches = small, over 30 inches = large, and everything in between (16–30 inches) = medium. Then they averaged the Snakebite Severity Scores (SSS) for each snake size class. SSS is a standardized method of scoring the seriousness of a pit viper bite, based on such factors as extent of swelling and bruising, respiratory distress, cardiac abnormalities, abnormal blood chemistry (primarily clotting problems), gastrointestinal abnormalities like nausea or diarrhea, central nervous system effects like headache, muscle weakness, twitching and seizures (Dart, et al., 1996). In general, SSS totals (range 0–20) of less than 2 are considered minimal severity, while scores over 8 are judged to be very severe.

Summarizing the findings of Janes, Bush and Kolluru (2010), while the average SSS produced by large rattlesnakes was slightly greater than the average produced by medium-sized rattlesnakes, the difference was not statistically significant, meaning that the difference was not greater than the margin of error. However, the average SSS produced by small rattlesnakes was statistically different at just over half of the average score produced by medium and large rattlesnakes.

The bottom line is this: large rattlesnakes can produce bites with only minor effects (or even dry bites) but very small rattlesnakes do not produce bites that are life- or limb-threatening. Think about it: laboratories that produce and sell venom for antivenom and research purposes do not want small snakes; they want big snakes because they produce a lot of venom.

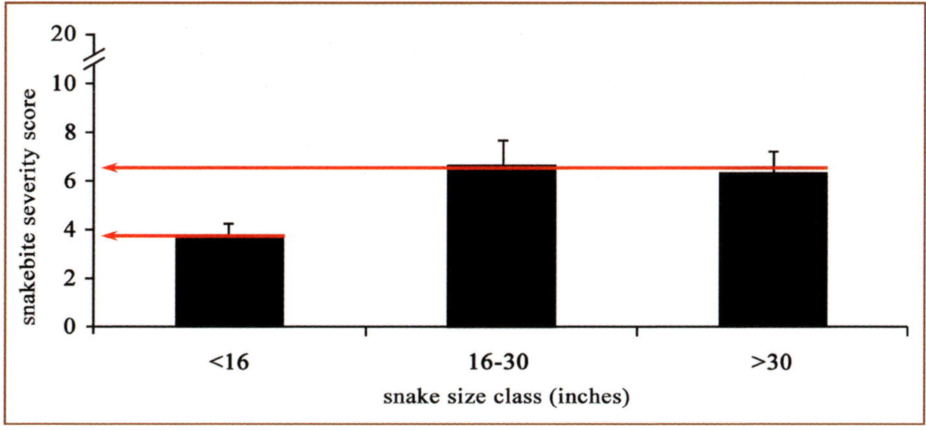

Average Snakebite Severity Scores, adapted from Janes, Bush and Kolluru, 2010.

MYTH #2 – RATTLESNAKES ARE RAPIDLY EVOLVING MORE TOXIC VENOM

False! From time to time, stories appear in the news media about rattlesnakes rapidly evolving more toxic venom – an idea often advanced by an emergency room physician who believes that he/she is seeing more severe snakebite cases than in years past. It has even been suggested that such rapid evolution is being caused by interactions between rattlesnakes and people. These beliefs were summarized in Natural History magazine (Grenard, 2000), suggesting that rampant hybridization between rattlesnake species, the killing of large rattlesnakes by people, an "arms race" between coevolving predators and prey, or a combination of these factors is producing increased neurotoxicity, requiring physicians to use much more antivenom to treat bites in recent years.

While there is no scientific evidence of such "rapid" evolution, despite many researchers studying snake venom at a molecular level, there are numerous persuasive arguments to the contrary. First, and perhaps most compelling, is the fact that natural selection is a painfully slow process, typically creating change in a population of animals over thousands of years – not a few decades. As summarized in Chapter 6, wild populations of hybrid rattlesnakes are extraordinarily rare and, where neurotoxic venoms are involved, the neurotoxicity typically does not spread beyond the hybrid zone.

What is evolving rapidly is our understanding of how to effectively treat rattlesnake bites and the realization that serious bites require lots of intravenous antivenom. It was just a few decades ago that bites were treated with one or two vials of antivenom injected into the muscle. As it became apparent that getting the antivenom into circulation rapidly was important, intravenous (IV) administration became the rule, followed by the realization that rapidly flooding the body with dozens of vials of antivenom was the best way to arrest the effects of a serious rattlesnake bite. So it is not so much that more antivenom is needed today compared to a few years ago, but rather that lots of antivenom has always been needed to treat seriously-envenomated bites and it has taken us years to figure that out. Drs. Bill Hayes and Steve Mackessy have eloquently refuted this myth (Hayes and Mackessy, 2010).

MYTH #3 – RATTLESNAKES ARE EVOLVING TO RATTLE LESS FREQUENTLY

False! People often ask me if rattlesnakes are evolving to rattle less and the rationale goes something like this: rattlesnakes that draw attention to themselves by rattling are killed by people, leaving the ones that don't rattle to survive and pass on those genes for not rattling. But that idea suggests a fundamental misunderstanding of evolution by natural selection. The number of rattlesnakes that interact with people is tiny compared to the entire population – the vast majority of which never encounter a person. And even if human encounters were more widespread and had the suggested effect, it would take much longer than a few decades for the genetic change to spread through the population.

MYTH #4 – RATTLESNAKES ARE AGGESSIVE TOWARDS PEOPLE

False! See Myth #2 in Chapter 10; Mohave Rattlesnake Myths. This applies to all rattlesnakes.

MYTH #5 – DROUGHT DRIVES RATTLESNAKES INTO POPULATED AREAS

False! It seems like an early summer tradition for the news media to proclaim that hot dry weather is driving rattlesnakes out of the foothills and into yards in search of water. And they invariably interview – not a herpetologist at a local university or a reptile curator at a zoo – but the owner of a "rattlesnake removal" service who poses with a menacing rattlesnake held aloft for the camera as he warns people to be alert because rattlesnakes are coming into yards looking for water.

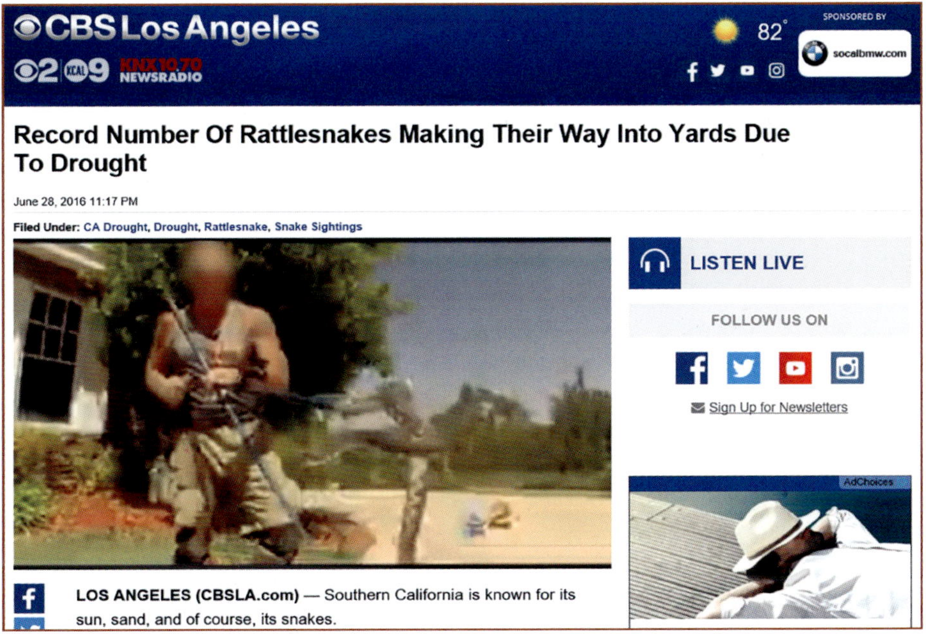
CBS Los Angeles
2 9 KNX 1070 NEWSRADIO
82°
SPONSORED BY socalbmw.com

Record Number Of Rattlesnakes Making Their Way Into Yards Due To Drought

June 28, 2016 11:17 PM

Filed Under: CA Drought, Drought, Rattlesnake, Snake Sightings

LISTEN LIVE

FOLLOW US ON

Sign Up for Newsletters

AdChoices

LOS ANGELES (CBSLA.com) — Southern California is known for its sun, sand, and of course, its snakes.

In fact, whether it is the Mediterranean Climate in California's foothills or the inland deserts of Arizona and Texas, the animals living there have evolved over millennia to survive and even thrive for months every year following the end of springtime rainfall. Small carnivores like rattlesnakes routinely do just fine on the body water of their prey (see Chapter 8). In fact, a severe drought occurred during the first year of my California field study of Mohave rattlesnakes, with no significant precipitation between January and November.

But did the rattlesnakes go wandering around looking for water during the drought? No! They modified their behavior to reduce water loss while continuing to hunt (remember, prey is 70% water). Movement was greatly reduced and reproductive activity stopped (i.e., males stopped searching for females) while both sexes protected much of their skin area by remaining coiled most of the time and often partially burying their coils in the soil (photo above) and they sheltered behind creosote bushes to escape wind and sun – all of which reduces evaporative water loss through the skin. Average daily movement during the drought was about 7 meters/day, compared to about 23 meters/day during 2003 and 2004, when precipitation returned to normal. Their home ranges were similarly reduced in size but they remained within their larger non-drought home ranges. They continued to gain water by ambushing prey animals while changing other behaviors to minimize water loss. But, importantly, they didn't go anywhere. Rather than moving more, they moved a lot less. (Cardwell, 2013)

In their natural environment, which is hot and bone dry for at least four or five months each summer, wandering around looking for non-existent water sources when they are water-stressed simply dehydrates rattlesnakes faster by exposing lots of skin to the hot dry air. And by crawling around, these obligatory sit-and-wait predators would also be giving up their primary water source – their ability to ambush prey.

The bottom line is this: drought that is locally severe enough to water-stress the rattlesnakes causes them to hunker down within their normal home range and move a lot less until conditions improve. Rattlesnakes found in yards (usually males looking for females) are very likely an indication that local conditions are not different enough from their usual hot dry summers to water-stress the snakes, despite low reservoir levels and reduced snow packs that make the news and worry people.

MYTH #6 – GIANT RATTLESNAKES

False! It is well accepted that the Eastern Diamondback (*Crotalus adamanteus*) is the largest of the rattlesnakes. According to Laurence Klauber, who collected voluminous records and correspondence about rattlesnakes from around the United States during the first half of the 20th century (when big rattlesnakes were far more common than in recent decades), the biggest eastern diamondback "report believed reliable" was 2,440 mm (a tiny fraction of an inch over 8 feet; Klauber, 1972:175). Klauber (1972:177) quotes a 1953 letter from E. Ross Allen of the Ross Allen Reptile Institute in Silver Springs, Florida:

> "I have been in business for nearly 28 years, during which time I have received from 1,000 to 5,000 *Crotalus adamanteus* annually, a total of about 50,000 altogether. The largest specimen I personally measured was 7 feet 3 inches in total length, exclusive of the rattle, and weighed 15 pounds. For years I offered a reward of $100 to anyone who brought in an 8-foot Florida diamondback, dead or alive. In recent years I have offered $200, without results. This reward still stands; I doubt that it will ever be claimed."

Klauber (1972:177) also states that specimens exceeding 7 feet are "well authenticated," although he never measured one himself. He also states that 8- and 9-foot animals have been reported, "possibly with some basis in truth."

Be suspicious of photos of "giant" snakes held out towards the camera. Using a technique called "close focus/wide angle," a photograph taken with a relatively wide angle lens makes the person holding the snake look smaller relative to the snake while both are in focus, making the snake appear much larger relative to the person in the photo.

By the way, the longest Mohave rattlesnake that is verifiable measured 48.7 inches total length. See Chapter 2: Description and Distribution.

Creosote bush (*Larrea tridentata*) scrub habitat in eastern Kern County, California, near the western limit of Mohave rattlesnake distribution. Mohave rattlesnakes and kangaroo rats favor sparse vegetation like this.

Avoiding Rattlesnake Bites 13

IDENTIFYING RATTLESNAKES

How do you identify a rattlesnake? I often hear about looking for triangular heads, elliptical "cat-like" pupils or the heat-sensitive facial pits that are peculiar to all pitvipers. It has always astonished me that so many people ignore the unique trait that gives rattlesnakes their name – the rattle!

Yes, rattlesnakes have triangular heads but some are less triangular than others and some harmless snakes also have triangular heads, especially when frightened and putting on a defensive display. Rattlesnakes do have elliptical pupils but some harmless snakes share this trait too. The heat-sensing facial pits are valid characters but the facial pits and pupil shape are far too small to see from a safe distance.

For safety, I always suggest staying at least twice the length of the snake away from a rattlesnake or any unidentified snake. So how do you reliably identify a rattlesnake from that distance? It's easy – look at the tail:

No rattlesnake has a long pointed tail!

Some harmless snakes have triangular heads, especially when frightened. This harmless gophersnake has just been accidentally stepped on by a hiker and is trying to look as intimidating as it can.

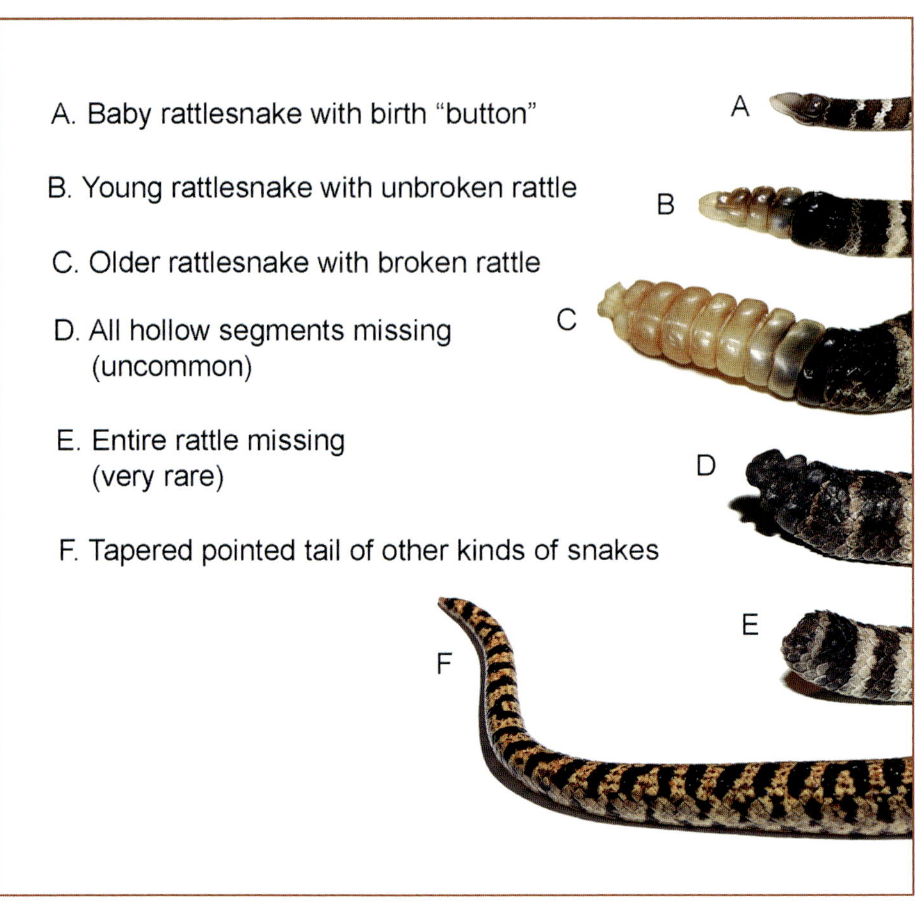

Of course, cottonmouths, copperheads, and coralsnakes have long pointed tails, but they are not found where Mohave rattlesnakes occur – except for the innocuous little Sonoran coralsnake (*Micruroides euryxanthus*) that does not produce medically significant envenomations. It is smaller, more brightly colored, and far less dangerous than coralsnakes in the southeastern United States.

Why twice the length of the snake? Because a rattlesnake cannot strike farther than its own length and, actually, probably somewhat less than that – especially defensively. But two-times the snake's length provides a nice buffer zone between you and the snake's longest possible reach. And staying out of reach is key; if you're too close, you just cannot react quickly enough if the snake strikes.

Depending on the species, newborn rattlesnakes are about 5 to 12 inches long and they are born with a small hard "button" at the end of the tail. Baby rattlesnakes are roughly the size of a pencil and the button is like the eraser. The button is small but you can safely look at a one-foot snake from two feet away – two-times its length.

The rattle is made of keratin – the same material as your hair and fingernails. As little rattlesnakes grow, the end of the tail slowly produces new rattle segments that are the same width as the tail. Since the tail gets wider as the snake gets bigger, the result is a tapered rattle with the oldest segment at the tip and the newest segment attached to the tail.

Over time, the older segments – including the first button – break off. Rattlesnakes that have reached adult size grow very slowly, if at all, so new rattle segments tend to be the same width as older ones. Thus, once the smaller tapered segments are gone, the rattle has a rectangular shape without any taper – indicating an older rattlesnake.

AVOIDING RATTLESNAKE BITES

Leave rattlesnakes alone! If you're not sure if it's a rattlesnake, leave it alone. Virtually all rattlesnake bites are the result of one of these two human activities: either putting unprotected hands or feet where you can't see or don't look, or intentionally bothering the snake.

Legitimate Bites

Bites by an undetected snake that is encountered by surprise are called "legitimate bites." Such bites occur when someone accidentally disturbs or startles an unseen rattlesnake. This can be as simple as accidentally stepping on a rattlesnake, especially at night on a porch or driveway. Rattlesnakes really dislike being stepped on! Reaching into and under plants while gardening is another common way to surprise a hidden rattlesnake.

Do they always rattle first? No. In fact, the first defense of a coiled rattlesnake is usually to sit still and hope they are not noticed. Stomping your feet or tapping ahead with a stick is of little value, since a coiled rattlesnake's response to nearby danger is usually to hunker down and not attract attention by moving. A rattlesnake that is already outstretched may flee into vegetation or down a nearby rodent burrow but you cannot count on that. Singing or making other noise is useless, as snakes have no ears. It's up to you to either be sure there is no rattlesnake where you put your hand or foot (or other body part!) or to wear protective clothing.

Remaining *at least* twice the apparent length of a rattlesnake away from the animal keeps people well beyond the reach of the snake's strike and provides a bit of an extra safety margin. Any closer risks a very nasty injury, not to mention an incredibly expensive hospital stay.

Covering the feet and ankles with leather shoes or hiking boots is a minimum for me, combined with long pants hanging down over and onto the boots. Of course, higher leather boots or even snake gaiters are much better protection but they can be expensive and uncomfortable…but I wear them when I'm radio-tracking rattlesnakes in vegetation that prevents me from seeing what I'm stepping on. Gloved hands are better than bare hands but only slightly, since glove leather is not nearly as thick and tough as shoe leather. Protect your hands with your eyes – look before you reach!

Illegitimate Bites

This is the term used for bites by a snake that has been discovered and then is intentionally bothered, leading to the bite. Many snakebite experts believe that the majority of cases showing up in hospital emergency rooms are illegitimate bites; that is, the interaction with the snake was not accidental. They happen as people try to kill or catch a rattlesnake, or make it rattle or strike, or even get a close-up photo of it. Regardless of the intent, making the decision to approach and interact with a rattlesnake sends the chances of being bitten through the roof. Turn and walk away and the chances of a bite are zero.

Finding a rattlesnake around your home can be an unsettling experience. Remember that choosing to interact with a rattlesnake for any reason dramatically increases the chance of a bite. If you must deal with a rattlesnake yourself, use a broom or other long-handled tool that keeps your hands and feet twice the length of the snake away from it. If you live in rattlesnake country, you must make a habit of looking where you are about to step or reach. Removing one rattlesnake does not remove the hazard, as my radiotelemetry studies have shown that they are often present in yards undetected.

An often repeated notion is that the "typical" snakebite patient is a young male adult who is intoxicated. Indeed, this is too often the case but experts disagree on the proportion of cases fitting this profile. Illegitimate bites also include bites by captive rattlesnakes, which are a whole different category of bites that are beyond the scope of this book. Over time, most captive rattlesnakes, including Mohaves, acclimate to captivity and lose their fear of people. But captive rattlesnakes are not pets! Indeed, since responsible keepers do not handle dangerous snakes, captive rattlesnakes soon learn that opening the cage door is usually associated with being fed. As a result, many bites to keepers by long-term captives are actually predatory bites by hungry rattlesnakes, rather than defensive bites. Add to that scenario the common practice of buying frozen mice or rats and constantly feeding thawed dead rodents to the snakes, and some snakes get very used to using little or no venom – adding even more uncertainty to what to expect following a captive rattlesnake bite.

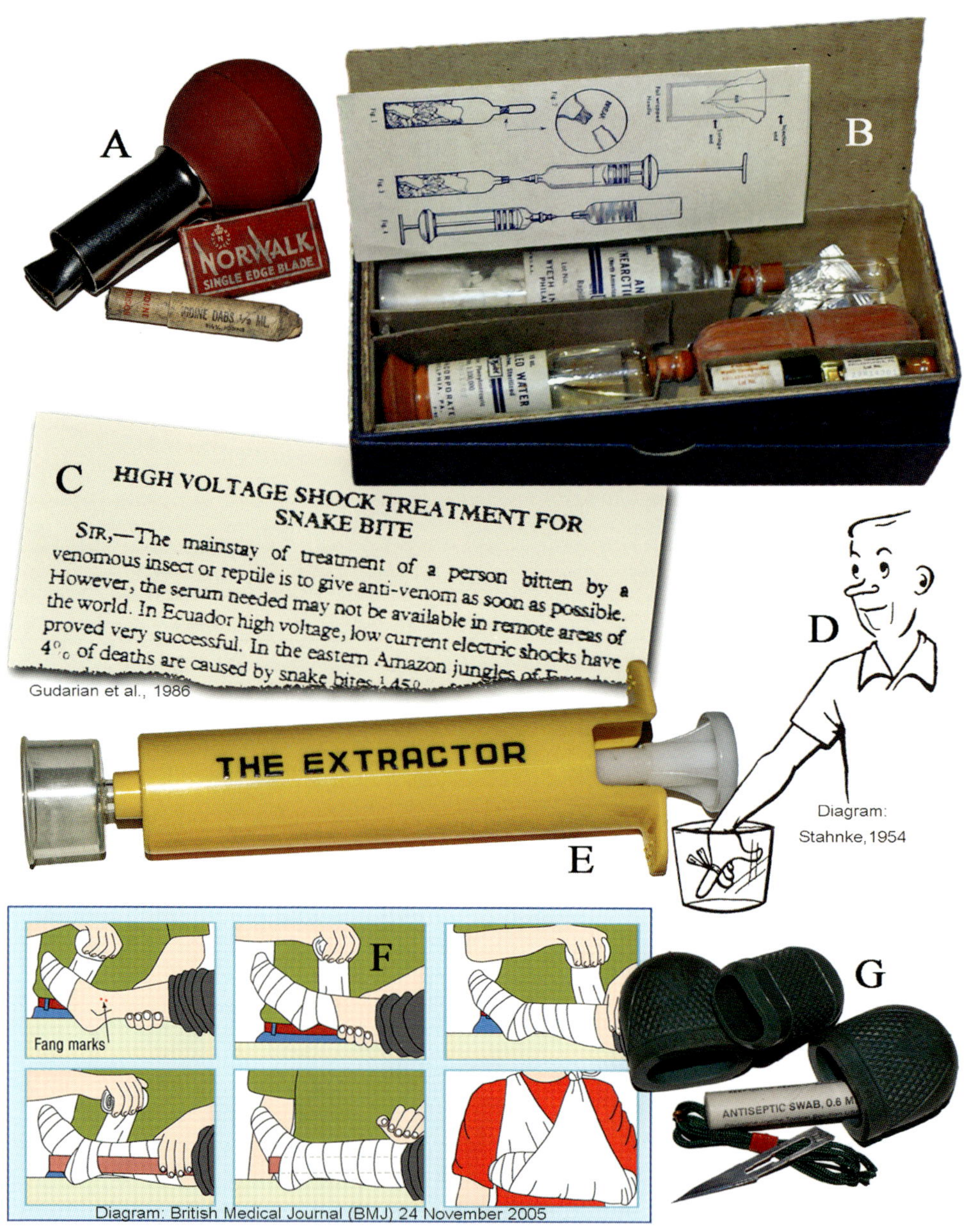

A sample of first aid devices and techniques suggested for rattlesnake bites in North America: Halco cut & suck kit, circa 1950s (A); Wyeth over-the-counter antivenin, including an early Cutter kit, circa 1950s (B); High voltage electricity, 1980s (C); Ligature & Cryotherapy, 1950s (D); Extractor® suction only device, 1970s–present (E); Pressure-Immobilization suggested by American Red Cross, 2010–present (F) and Cutter cut & suck kit, circa 1960 (G). Not shown: Tourniquets, the oldest method and included in many of the 20th century kits.

14 First-Aid for Rattlesnake Bites

In the event of a rattlesnake bite, the victim should be safely transported without delay to the nearest hospital emergency room. Period!

It makes no difference if it is a Mohave rattlesnake or some other species. The Wilderness Medical Society's 2015 revision of the treatment guidelines for North American pitviper bites (of which I was a coauthor) states:

> "There is nothing that can be done in the field to significantly alter the outcome of a serious snakebite, and field first aid should not delay rapid transfer to a facility capable of safely administering antivenom."
>
> (Kanaan et al., 2015:476)

How can you tell right away if a rattlesnake bite is going to be a "serious" bite? You can't. And waiting to see if it gets worse before seeking medical attention is a very bad idea. Find out how serious it is – or isn't – in the emergency room.

Depending on your location, you're best snakebite kit will be either your cell phone or your car keys. Most rattlesnake bites do not happen in remote places. Where paramedic services are available, call "911" and let them transport the bitten person. Paramedics are most likely to get the victim to a hospital quickly and safely, while avoiding hospitals swamped by patients from some other emergency or a hospital that just used its small stock of antivenom on another recent snakebite.

If local paramedics are not available or there is no phone service, drive the victim safely to either a hospital or to a location with cellular service, if that will allow a call to paramedics. I am often asked what to do if someone is alone and bitten in a wilderness location without phone service. I can only tell you what I would do and that is to walk out, either to my car or to a place where I can get a phone signal and call for help. My own opinion is that a rattlesnake bite in a remote area is well worth a helicopter evacuation, if one can be arranged.

So why is rapid transportation to a medical facility so important? Because antivenom cannot repair cellular damage that has already occurred, it can only neutralize venom that has not yet found its target tissue. And venom begins destroying tissue immediately after the bite, although it may not become obvious for a while. As snakebite docs are fond of saying, "Time is tissue!"

A recently published attempt to identify early factors that are likely to predict a serious envenomation analyzed clinical data from 17 earlier snakebite studies involving 5,915 patients (Gerardo et al., 2019). After exhaustive analysis, the authors identified four factors, the presence of any one of which significantly increased the likelihood of severe systemic envenomation:

Time from bite to medical care longer than six hours
Patient age younger than twelve years
Large snake size
Ptosis (drooping eyelids)

The authors were careful to point out that absence of these factors is not necessarily reassuring, as severe envenomations often occur in adults who reach medical care right away after being bitten by average-sized snakes. Also note that ptosis, an early sign of systemic neurotoxicity, will not be present following even severe envenomations by most North American pitvipers because so few of them have significant neurotoxic components in their venom. Obvious exceptions are venom-A Mohave rattlesnakes (See Chapter 9). But even with a neurotoxic bite, ptosis and other neurological defects may not become apparent for several hours.

WHAT TO EXPECT AT THE EMERGENCY ROOM

Snakebite is not a topic routinely covered in medical school, nor are doctors likely to see snakebites during their residency program. And most practicing physicians have never treated a snakebite. The good news is that most physicians are also bright resourceful professionals who seek advice when necessary and the nation's poison control centers have, for the most part, become very good at putting them in touch with other clinicians who are true snakebite experts. But doctors are human and they hear and read the same misinformation about rattlesnakes and snakebite as the rest of us.

So what should you be alert for when you reach medical care? A rattlesnake bite is a medical emergency and time to effective treatment is critical. You should not have to wait for triage in the waiting room. Not all rattlesnake bites need antivenom but that determination needs to be made without delay. Swelling progressing away from the bite site is cause for concern. Blood coagulation problems are a common result of serious rattlesnake bites and blood should be drawn and sent to the lab right away to look for early signs.

If significant signs or symptoms of envenomation are present, antivenom is likely indicated. And if antivenom is needed, the sooner it is started, the more effective it will be.

Some physicians are shy about using antivenom because of concerns about a sudden life-threatening allergic reaction to it. These concerns are probably just left over from the old Wyeth antivenom days; current pitviper antivenoms available in the United States are much safer. And the snakebite docs with whom I am familiar are able to safely administer antivenom, even to an allergic patient.

My last caution is regarding surgery for your rattlesnake bite. Snake-bitten appendages can swell to grotesque proportions and some emergency medicine physicians, used to treating other trauma but not rattlesnake bites, sometimes conclude that emergency surgery is necessary to save the limb. The procedure, called "fasciotomy," opens the entire limb surgically to relieve pressure and preserve blood flow. But snakebite specialists whom I know and conference with believe that fasciotomy is very seldom, if ever, indicated for a rattlesnake bite because most swelling is superficial and even deep swelling can be reversed with enough antivenom. (Kanaan et al., 2015:481; Gold et al., 2003)

If you find yourself concerned about the treatment you are (or are not) receiving following a rattlesnake bite, consider demanding that your doctor consult with a snakebite expert. This can be accomplished by contacting the National Poison Center Hotline at 800-222-1222. Living in Tucson, I am lucky to have the Arizona Poison and Drug Information Center and associated Banner-University Medical Center nearby, home to some of the most qualified snakebite experts in the world. I carry their phone number around with me.

ANTIVENOM

Antivenom products used to treat snakebites are actually freeze dried antibodies harvested from horses or sheep that have been hyper-immunized against snake venoms by repeated small harmless doses of venom. Once the sheep or horses achieve a very high titer of the desired antibodies, blood is harmlessly drawn periodically and the antibodies are separated, freeze dried, and packaged as antivenom.

Antivenom has come a long way in the United States over the past seventy years. Between the late 1940s and 2000, the only product available in the United States to treat rattlesnake envenomations was Antivenin (Crotalidae) Polyvalent, made by Wyeth Laboratories. While it saved many lives and limbs, it was far from a pure preparation and it included the entire horse antibody molecule, which was recognized in humans as a foreign protein and thus produced frequent allergic reactions that were sometimes life-threatening.

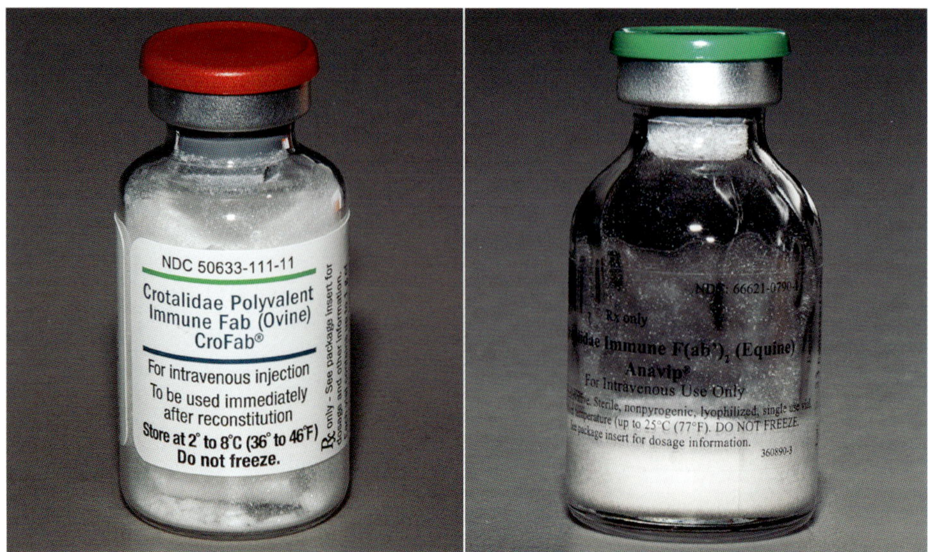

CroFab® antivenom by BTG (left) and AnaVip® antivenom by Instituto Bioclon via Rare Disease Therapeutics (right).

CroFab®, originally sold by Protherics (now BTG), became available in 2000 and remains available at this writing. It is a much purer preparation of antibodies raised in sheep and the antibody molecule is cleaved to separate the two active sites from the molecule while washing away the molecular "tail" that identifies it as a sheep protein. CroFab® has proven to be far less allergenic than the Wyeth product and one of the four venoms used to create antibodies in the sheep is Mohave rattlesnake venom-A, making it a specific antivenom for neurotoxic Mohaves. Venoms from other species used to create antibodies for CroFab® cover the toxins in other rattlesnake species, including those produced by venom-B Mohaves.

However, CroFab® has had two problems: price and "recurrence syndrome." Patients have sometimes been billed more than $10,000/vial for CroFab®, with a critical bite sometimes taking as many as 40–50 vials. CroFab® is also eliminated from the body by the kidneys much faster than the whole-molecule Wyeth antivenom, requiring more antivenom to keep the envenomation syndrome in check until all the venom has been neutralized.

Finally, in October 2018, AnaVip® became available in the United States. Made in Mexico by Instituto Bioclon, AnaVip® is a horse-derived product in which the allergenic tail of the antibody molecule is removed but the two active sites remain connected to one another. This molecular configuration reduces the potential for allergy while keeping the molecule in the blood longer, reducing or eliminating the recurrence syndrome seen with CroFab®. It is also expected to be less expensive, and early clinical experience suggests that treatment with AnaVip® may run about half the price of CroFab®. Although Mohave rattlesnake venom is not used in the preparation of AnaVip®, it contains antibodies raised against venom from the tropical rattlesnake (*Crotalus durissus*), which contains a pre-synaptic neurotoxin almost identical to Mohave venom–A and the resulting antibodies cross-neutralize very well.

HISTORIC FIRST AID MEASURES NOW DISCREDITED

The past half century has seen a bewildering array of snakebite first aid techniques suggested and later rejected by experts. None of these techniques or devices have been shown to remove much, if any, venom – despite manufacturers' claims. Some have been shown to cause additional injury. And all waste time that should be used to reach antivenom.

Tourniquets have been recognized as useful to prevent the spread of venoms from the bite site for centuries but the dangers of tourniquets have been evident for just as long. Tourniquets do nothing to slow tissue destruction and, left on too long, produce tissue death and subsequent gangrene, causing loss of the limb and often loss of the patient's life. They can be far more dangerous than North American rattlesnake bites.

Antivenom for field use was available in the 1950s and 60s. A person could buy Wyeth Antivenin (Crotalidae) Polyvalent (ACP) over the counter and carry it around for immediate personal use. In the booklet produced by Wyeth (Wyeth Laboratories, 1965:22), it is stated that "In an acute emergency, in which severe symptoms... develop rapidly, and medical aid cannot be promptly obtained, the serum may be administered by a layman, and may even be self-injected if imperative."

I do not have the date when Wyeth ACP was withdrawn from over-the-counter sales but by 1980, snakebite references commonly acknowledged the danger of immediate life-threatening anaphylaxis and referred to ACP being administered only by physicians in a hospital setting with anti-allergy drugs at bedside (summarized by Russell, 1980:311-314). Even after paramedics began to bring advanced life-saving procedures and drugs to patients in the field, ACP was not included in the paramedics' kit. This was partly due to the danger of anaphylaxis but also because ACP takes precious minutes to reconstitute from its freeze-dried state and a large percentage of snakebite victims arrive at a hospital as fast as the antivenom can be reconstituted and administered.

Cut and suck kits were popular when I was young and are still available. Consisting of some variation of suction devices, a scalpel blade and usually a chord for use as a tourniquet or "constriction band" and sometimes some antiseptic. They usually also include some instructions for cutting into the fang punctures before applying suction. Besides being ineffective at removing venom, a panicked first aid provider can do a lot of damage with a razor blade, including to nerves, tendons, and blood vessels.

Ice and ice water immersion was popularized in the 1950s as a way of arresting the action of various venoms (snake, spider, scorpion, etc.), as well as slowing the perceived growth of bacteria in an envenomed wound. Pitched as being "effective against any type of envenomization" (Stahnke, 1954:3) and combining a temporary tight ligature with prolonged "cryotherapy," the "L-C Technique" (Ligature-Cryotherapy) involved trapping the venom in the affected appendage with a ligature until the limb could be immersed in ice water and cooled, after which the ligature was to be removed. It took ten years for reports of tissue death and permanent disability resulting from prolonged ice water immersion to accumulate and eventually be published (summarized by Russell, 1980:275–276).

The application of ice, icepacks, ice water, or freezing chemicals to snakebites is no longer advocated and, in fact, is now broadly discouraged.

Suction only devices are usually spring-loaded syringe-shaped gadgets designed to be placed over the fang punctures without first cutting the skin. While popular and still broadly available, multiple studies have failed to demonstrate the ability of suction devices to remove venom, including a study at Loma Linda University in 2000 where we found that the device apparently concentrated the venom under the suction cup sufficiently to produce tissue death and necrosis, while no tissue injury occurred without suction (Bush et al., 2000).

Electric shock sprang upon the snakebite community as a potential remedy in 1986 with a report in the British medical journal *Lancet*. It reported the successful treatment of pitviper envenomations in Ecuador with high voltage, low amperage, electric shocks produced by an outboard motor spark plug wire (Guderian et al., 1986). Even though all subsequent efforts to validate this technique failed (e.g., Johnson et al., 1987), some makers of defensive "stun guns" marketed their devices for snakebite first aid for some time thereafter.

Compression wraps and "Pressure Immobilization". Rattlesnake bites almost always deposit the venom in the skin or in the fatty subcutaneous layer under the skin. As a result, application of a compression wrap (i.e., an elastic or crepe bandage) over the bite site has the potential to sequester the venom at the bite. "Pressure-immobilization" (PI) was developed in Australia for snakebite first aid where many snakes produce deadly neurotoxic venom without tissue-destroying properties (Sutherland et al., 1979).

Snakebite experts in the United States have always been reluctant to suggest compression wraps or PI for native pitviper bites because the major result of these bites is tissue damage around the bite site (deaths are rare) and trapping the venom at the bite is very likely to worsen such damage. I was even involved in a study at Loma Linda University where we demonstrated that PI significantly raises pressure in the envenomed tissue beneath the wrap, which is likely to increase tissue damage (Bush et al., 2004). Yet, in 2010, the American Heart Association (AHA) and the American Red Cross (ARC) surprised everyone in their routine five-year first aid update by advocating PI for bites by "non-neurotoxic American snakes" (Markenson et al., 2010:S938). They based their recommendation on two references: a coralsnake paper (which is a neurotoxic snake) and our 2004 Loma Linda study (Bush et al., 2004).

The authors of the 2004 Loma Linda study wrote a letter disagreeing with the PI recommendation and complaining that we had not recommended PI but the AHA and ARC refused to change their position. The following year, the major professional toxicology societies got together and published a position paper in the journal *Clinical Toxicology*, concluding:

> "Available evidence fails to establish the efficacy of pressure immobilization in humans, but indicates the possibility of serious adverse events arising from its use. The use of pressure immobilization for the pre-hospital treatment of North American Crotalinae envenomation is not recommended."
>
> American College of Medical Toxicology et al. (2011:882)

Nonetheless, although pressure-immobilization is generally not utilized in the United States, the PI recommendation for North American pitviper bites by the American Heart Association and the American Red Cross remains in effect as this book goes to press.

Literature Cited

Aldridge, R.D., and D. Duvall (2002). Evolution of the mating season in the pitvipers of North America. Herpetological Monographs 16:1–25.

American College of Medical Toxicology, American Academy of Clinical Toxicology, American Association of Poison Control Centers, European Association of Poison Control Centres and Clinical Toxicologists, International Society on Toxinology, and Asia Pacific Association of Medical Toxicology (2011). Pressure immobilization after North American Crotalinae snake envenomation. Clinical Toxicology 49:881–882. doi:10.3109/15563650.2011.610802

Anonymous (1965). Dr. Shannon's tragic death is shock to the community. The Wickenburg Sun Newspaper. 2 September 1965:1.

Bieber, A.L., T. Tu, and A.T. Tu (1975). Studies of an acidic cardiotoxin isolated from the venom of Mojave Rattlesnake (*Crotalus scutulatus*). Biochimica et Biophysica Acta 400:178–188.

Bush, S.P., and M.D. Cardwell (1999). Mojave Rattlesnake (*Crotalus scutulatus scutulatus*) Identification. Wilderness and Environmental Medicine 10:6–9.

Bush, S.P., S.M. Green, T.A. Laack, W.K. Hayes, M.D. Cardwell, and D.A. Tanen (2004). Pressure immobilization delays mortality and increases intracompartmental pressure after artificial intramuscular rattlesnake envenomation in a porcine model. Annals of Emergency Medicine 44:599–604.

Bush, S.P., K.G. Hegewald, S.M. Green, M.D. Cardwell, and W.K. Hayes (2000). Effects of a negative pressure venom extraction device (Extractor) on local tissue injury after artificial rattlesnake envenomation in a porcine model. Wilderness and Environmental Medicine 11:180–188.

Bush, S.P., E.T. Teacher, L. Daniel-Underwood, S.R. Pearl, J. Westeren, T.H. Phan, and E. Reibling (2012). Combined neurotoxicity and hematotoxicity with clinically significant bleeding after Mohave rattlesnake (*Crotalus scutulatus*) envenoming in southern California. Toxicon 60:218.

Campbell, J.A. and W.W. Lamar (2004). The Venomous Reptiles of the Western Hemisphere, 2 vols. Comstock Publishing, Ithaca, New York.

Cardwell, M.D. (2005). *Crotalus scutulatus* (Mohave Rattlesnake). Natural History Notes. Behavior. Herpetological Review 36:192.

Cardwell, M.D. (2006). Rain-harvesting in a wild population of *Crotalus s. scutulatus* (Serpentes: Viperidae). Herpetological Review 37:142–144.

Cardwell, M.D. (2008). The reproductive ecology of Mohave rattlesnakes. Journal of Zoology 274:65–76.

Cardwell, M.D. (2013). Behavioral changes by Mohave Rattlesnakes (*Crotalus scutulatus*) in response to drought. Unpublished thesis, California State University, Sacramento, California. (available at http://csus-dspace.calstate.edu/handle/10211.9/2063)

Cardwell, M.D. (2016). Species Accounts. Mohave Rattlesnake *Crotalus scutulatus* (Kennicott 1861). Pp. 563–605 *In* G.W. Schuett, M.J. Feldner, C.F. Smith, and R.S. Reiserer (Eds.), Rattlesnakes of Arizona, vol. 1. ECO Publishing, Rodeo, New Mexico.

Cardwell, M.D., and B. Alexander (2006). *Crotalus scutulatus scutulatus* (Mohave Rattlesnake). Albinism. Herpetological Review 37:477.

Cardwell, M.D., and J. Banashek (2006). *Crotalus scutulatus scutulatus* (Mohave Rattlesnake). Morphology. Herpetological Review 37:477.

Cardwell, M.D., S.W. Gotte, R.W. McDiarmid, N. Gilmore and J.A. Poindexter (2013). Type specimen of *Crotalus scutulatus* (Chordata: Reptilia: Squamata: Viperidae) re-examined, with new evidence after more than a century of confusion. Proceedings of the Biological Society of Washington 126:11–16.

Conant, R. (1975). A Field Guide to Reptiles and Amphibians of Eastern and Central North America. Houghton Mifflin, Boston, Massachusetts.

Conant, R., F.R. Cagle, C.J. Goin, C.H. Lowe, W.T. Neill, M.G. Netting, K.P. Schmidt, C.E. Shaw, and R.C. Stebbins (1956). Common names for North American amphibians and reptiles. Copeia 1956:172–185.

Conant, R., and J.T. Collins (1998). A Field Guide to Reptiles & Amphibians of Eastern and Central North America, (3rd ed.). Houghton Mifflin, Boston, Massachusetts.

Cope, E.D. (1900). The crocodilians, lizards, and snakes of North America. Pp.153–1270 + 36 pls. *In* Report of the U.S. National Museum for the Year Ending June 30, 1898. Government Printing Office, Washington, D.C.

Crother, B.I. (Ed.) (2000) [published 2001]. Scientific and Standard English Names of Amphibians and Reptiles of North America North of Mexico, with Comments Regarding Confidence in Our Understanding, (5th ed). Herpetological Circular #29, Society for the Study of Amphibians and Reptiles.

Crother, B.I. (Ed.) (2003). Scientific and standard English names of amphibians and reptiles of North America North of Mexico: Update. Herpetological Review 34:196–203.

Crother, B.I. (Ed.) (2008). Scientific and Standard English Names of Amphibians and Reptiles of North America North of Mexico, with Comments Regarding Confidence in our Understanding, (6th ed). Herpetological Circular #37, Society for the Study of Amphibians and Reptiles.

Crother, B.I. (Ed.) (2012). Scientific and Standard English and French Names of Amphibians and Reptiles of North America North of Mexico, with Comments Regarding Confidence in our Understanding, (7th ed). Herpetological Circular #39, Society for the Study of Amphibians and Reptiles.

Crother, B.I. (Ed.) (2017). Scientific and Standard English Names of Amphibians and Reptiles of North America North of Mexico, with Comments Regarding Confidence in our Understanding, (8th ed). Herpetological Circular #43, Society for the Study of Amphibians and Reptiles.

Dart, R.C., K.M. Hurlbut, R. Garcia, and J. Boren (1996). Validation of a severity score for the assessment of Crotalid snakebite. Annals of Emergency Medicine 27:321–326.

Davis, M.A., M.J. Feldner and G.W. Schuett (2016). Species Accounts. Arizona Black Rattlesnake *Crotalus cerberus* (Coues 1875). Pp. 109–178 *In* G.W. Schuett, M.J. Feldner, C.F. Smith and R.S. Reiserer (Eds.), Rattlesnakes of Arizona, vol. 1. ECO Publishing, Rodeo, New Mexico.

Degenhardt, W.G., C.W. Painter, and A.H. Price. (1996). Amphibians and Reptiles of New Mexico. University of New Mexico Press, Albuquerque, New Mexico

De Lisle, H.F. (2017). Amphibians and Reptiles of Joshua Tree National Park. (2nd ed.) Self-published by the author. (Available at: www.researchgate.net/publication/312589252_Amphibians_Reptiles_Joshua_Tree_NP_Second_edition)

Ernst, C.H., and E.M. Ernst (2003). Snakes of the United States and Canada. Smithsonian Books, Washington, D.C.

Ernst, C.H., and E.M. Ernst (2012). Venomous Reptiles of the United States, Canada, and Northern Mexico, 2 vols. Johns Hopkins University Press, Baltimore, Maryland.

Fahey, J.H. (2015). More than "The Fighting Doctor": Brigadier General Bernard J. D. Irwin. Military Medicine 180:1116–1117.

Fahey, J.H. (2017). Fort Buchanan and the origins of Arizona Territory. Journal of Arizona History 58:111–156.

Forrester, J.A., T.G. Weiser and J.D. Forrester (2018). An update on fatalities from venomous and non-venomous animals in the United States (2008–2015). Wilderness and Environmental Medicine 29:36–44.

Gerardo, C.J., J.R.N. Vissoci, C.S. Evans, D.L. Simel, and E.J. Lavonas (2019). Does my patient have a severe snake envenomation? JAMA Surgery. doi:10.1001/jamasurg.2018.5069.

Glenn, J.L., and R. Straight (1978). Mojave rattlesnake *Crotalus scutulatus scutulatus* venom: variation in toxicity with geographical origin. Toxicon 16:81–84.

Glenn, J.L., and R.C. Straight (1982). The rattlesnakes and their venom yield and lethal toxicity. *In* A.T. Tu (Ed.). Rattlesnake Venoms, Their Actions and Treatment. Marcel Dekker, New York.

Glenn, J.L., and R.C. Straight (1990). Venom characteristics as an indicator of hybridization between *Crotalus viridis viridis* and *Crotalus scutulatus scutulatus* in New Mexico. Toxicon 28:857–862.

Gloyd, H.K. (1940). The Rattlesnakes, Genera *Sistrurus* and *Crotalus*. Chicago Academy of Sciences, Special Publication No. 4, Chicago, Illinois.

Gold, B.S., R.A. Barish, R.C. Dart, R.P. Silverman, and G. V. Bochicchio (2003). Resolution of compartment syndrome after rattlesnake envenomation utilizing non-invasive measures. Journal of Emergency Medicine 24:285–288.

Goldberg, S.R., and P.C. Rosen (2000). Reproduction in the Mojave rattlesnake, *Crotalus scutulatus* (Serpentes: Viperidae). Texas Journal of Science 52:101–109.

Grenard, S. (2000). Is rattlesnake venom evolving? Natural History Magazine July-August:44–49.

Guderian, R.H., C.D. Mackenzie, and J.F. Williams (1986). High voltage shock treatment for snake bite. (letter) Lancet 2:229 (July 26).

Hardy, D.L. (1983). Envenomation by the Mojave rattlesnake (*Crotalus scutulatus scutulatus*) in southern Arizona, U.S.A. Toxicon 21:111–118.

Hardy, D.L. (1985). Rattlesnake envenomation in Tucson, Arizona: 1973-1980. (abstract) Toxicon 23:573.

Hardy, D.L. (1986). Fatal rattlesnake envenomations in Arizona: 1969-1984. Clinical Toxicology 24:1–10.

Hayes, W.K., and S.P. Mackessy (2010). Sensationalistic journalism and tales of snakebite: Are rattlesnakes rapidly evolving more toxic venom? Wilderness and Environmental Medicine 21:35–45.

Herbert, S.S., and W.K. Hayes (2008). Venom expenditure by rattlesnakes and killing effectiveness in rodent prey: Do rattlesnakes expend optimal amounts of venom? Pp. 221–228 *In* W.K. Hayes, K.R. Beaman, M.D. Cardwell, and S.P. Bush (Eds.), The Biology of Rattlesnakes. Loma Linda University Press, Loma Linda, California.

Jacob, J.S. (1977). An evaluation of the possibility of hybridization between the rattlesnakes *Crotalus atrox* and *C. scutulatus* in the southwestern United States. Southwestern Naturalist 22:469–485.

Jaeger, E.C. (1957). The North American Deserts. Stanford University Press, Stanford, California.

Janes D.N., S.P. Bush, and G.R. Kolluru (2010). Large snake size suggests increased snakebite severity in patients bitten by rattlesnakes in southern California. Wilderness and Environmental Medicine 21:120–126.

Johnson, E., K. Kardong, and S. Mackessy (1987). Electric shocks are ineffective in treatment of lethal effects of rattlesnake envenomation in mice. Toxicon 25:1347–1349.

Jones, L.L.C. (2016). Spelling of the word "Mojave" vs. "Mohave" as it relates to standard English names for reptiles. Sonoran Herpetologist 29:65–71.

Kanaan, N.C., J. Ray, M. Stewart, K.W. Russell, M. Fuller, S.P. Bush, E.M. Caravati, M.D. Cardwell, R.L. Norris, and S.A. Weinstein (2015). Wilderness Medical Society practice guidelines for the treatment of pitviper envenomations in the United States. Wilderness & Environmental Medicine 26:472–487.

Kelly, A. (1909). A Yuma rattler. Forest and Stream 30 October 1909:691.

Kennicott, R. (1861). On three new forms of rattlesnakes. Proceedings of the Academy of Natural Sciences of Philadelphia 13:206–208.

Klauber, L.M. (1930). New and renamed subspecies of *Crotalus confluentus* Say, with remarks on related species. Transactions of the San Diego Society of Natural History VI:95–144.

Klauber, L.M. (1956). Rattlesnakes – Their Habits, Life Histories and Influence on Mankind, 2 Vols. University of California Press, Los Angeles and Berkeley, California.

Klauber, L.M. (1972). Rattlesnakes – Their Habits, Life Histories and Influence on Mankind, 2 Vols. (2nd ed.) University of California Press, Los Angeles and Berkeley, California.

Lowe, C.H., C.R. Schwalbe, and T.B. Johnson (1986). The Venomous Reptiles of Arizona. Arizona Game and Fish Department, Phoenix, Arizona.

Mackessy, S.P. (2008). Venom composition in rattlesnakes: trends and biological significance. Pp. 459–510 *In* W.K. Hayes, K.R. Beaman, M.D. Cardwell, and S.P.

Bush (Eds.), The Biology of Rattlesnakes. Loma Linda University Press, Loma Linda, California.

Mackessy, S.P. (2010a). Evolutionary trends in venom composition in the Western Rattlesnakes (*Crotalus viridis* sensu lato): Toxicity vs. tenderizers. Toxicon 55:1463–1474.

Mackessy, S.P. (2010b). The field of reptile toxinology: snakes, lizards, and their venoms. Pp. 3–24 *In* S.P. Mackessy. (Ed.) Handbook of Venoms and Toxins of Reptiles. CRC Press, Boca Raton, Florida.

Mackessy, S.P., and T.A. Castoe (2016). Deciphering the evolution of venom and the venom apparatus in rattlesnakes. Pp. 57–90 *In* G.W. Schuett, M.J. Feldner, C.F. Smith and R.S. Reiserer (Eds.). Rattlesnakes of Arizona, vol. 2. ECO Publishing, Rodeo, New Mexico.

Marchant, J.R.V., and J.F. Charles (1957). Cassell's Latin Dictionary. Funk and Wagnalls, New York, New York.

Markenson, D., J.D. Ferguson, L. Chameides, P. Cassan, K. Chung, J. Epstein, L. Gonzales, R. A. Herrington, J.L. Pellegrino, N. Ratcliff, and S. Singer (2010). 2010 American Heart Association and American Red Cross Guidelines for First Aid (Part 17: First Aid). Circulation 122:S934–S946. doi:10.1161/circulationaha.110.971150

Massey, D.J., J.J. Calvete, E.E. Sanchez, L. Sanz, K. Richards, R. Curtis, and K. Boesen (2012). Venom variability and envenoming severity outcomes of the *Crotalus scutulatus scutulatus* (Mojave rattlesnake) from Southern Arizona. Proteomics 75:2576–2587.

McDiarmid, R.W., J.A. Campbell, and T. Touré (1999). Snake Species of the World. A Taxonomic and Geographic Reference, vol. 1. The Herpetologists' League, Washington, D. C.

Mrinalini, J.J. Hicks, and W. Wüster (2015). Natural History Notes. *Crotalus scutulatus* (Mohave Rattlesnake). Maximum size. Herpetological Review 46:271.

Murphy, R.W., and C.B. Crabtree (1988). Genetic identification of a natural hybrid rattlesnake: *Crotalus scutulatus scutulatus* x *C. viridis viridis*. Herpetologica 44: 119–123.

Nagy, K.A. (1987). How do desert animals get enough water? Pp. 89–98 *In* L. Berkofsky and M. G. Wurtele (Eds.), Progress in Desert Research, Rowman and Littlefield, Totowa, New Jersey.

Norris, R.L., S.P. Bush and M.D. Cardwell (2015). Bites by venomous reptiles in Canada, the United States, and Mexico. Pp. 729–759 *In* P.S. Auerbach (Ed), Auerbach's Wilderness Medicine (7th ed.), Elsevier, Philadelphia, Pennsylvania.

Pope, C.H. (1937). Snakes Alive and How They Live. Viking Press, New York.

Price, A.H. (2009). Venomous Snakes of Texas. University of Texas Press, Austin.

Reyes-Velasco, J., J.M. Meik, E.N. Smith, and T.A. Castoe (2013). Phylogenetic relationships of the enigmatic longtailed rattlesnakes (*Crotalus ericsmithi*, *C. lannomi*, and *C. stejnegeri*). Molecular Phylogenetics and Evolution 69:524–534.

Russell, F.E. (1980). Snake Venom Poisoning. Scholium International, Great Neck, New York.

Schield, D.R., R.H. Adams, D.C. Card, A.B. Corbin, T. Jezkova, N.R. Hales, J.M. Meik, B.W. Perry, C.L. Spencer, L.L. Smith, G.C. García, N.M. Bouzid, J.L. Strickland, C.L. Parkinson, M. Borja, G. Castañeda-Gaytán, R.W. Bryson Jr., O.A. Flores-Villela, S.P. Mackessy, and T.A. Castoe (2018). Cryptic genetic diversity, population structure, and gene flow in the Mojave rattlesnake (*Crotalus scutulatus*). Molecular Phylogenetics and Evolution 127:669–681.

Schuett, G.W. (1992). Is long-term sperm storage an important component of the reproductive biology of temperate pitvipers? Pp. 169–184 *In* J.A. Campbell and E.D. Brodie, Jr. (Eds.), Biology of the Pitvipers. Selva, Tyler, Texas.

Schuett, G.W., S.L. Carlisle, A.T. Holycross, J.K. O'Leile, D.L. Hardy Sr., E.A. Van Kirk, and W.J. Murdoch (2002). Mating system of male Mojave Rattlesnakes (*Crotalus scutulatus*): Seasonal timing of mating, agonistic behavior, spermatogenesis, sexual segment of the kidney, and plasma sex steroids, Pp. 515–532 *In* G.W. Schuett, M.Höggren, M.E. Douglas and H.W. Greene (Eds.), Biology of the Vipers. Eagle Mountain Publishing, Eagle Mountain, Utah.

Sherer, L.M. (1967). The name Mojave, Mohave: A history of its origin and meaning. Southern California Quarterly 49:1–36.

Smith, H.M., and F.E. Russell (1965). Frederick Albert Shannon 1921–1965. Copeia 1965:541–542.

Smith, H.M. and E.H. Taylor (1945). An annotated checklist and key to the snakes of Mexico. United States National Museum Bulletin 187, U.S. Government Printing Office, Washington, D.C.

Smith, H.M. and E.H. Taylor (1950). Type localities of Mexican reptiles and amphibians. The University of Kansas Science Bulletin 33:313–380.

Smith, J., and S. Bush (2010). Envenomations by reptiles in the United States. Pp. 475–490 *In* S.P. MacKessy (Ed.), Handbook of Venoms and Toxins of Reptiles. CRC Press, Boca Raton, Florida.

Stahnke, H.L. (1954). The L-C Method of Treating Venomous Bites and Stings. Self-published by the author, Tempe, Arizona.

Stebbins, R.C. (1985). A Field Guide to Western Reptiles and Amphibians (2nd ed.). Houghton Mifflin, Boston, Massachusetts.

Stebbins, R.C. (2003). A Field Guide to Western Reptiles and Amphibians (3rd ed.). Houghton Mifflin, Boston, Massachusetts.

Stebbins, R.C., and S.M. McGinnis (2012). Field Guide to Amphibians and Reptiles of California (Revised ed.). University of California Press, Berkeley.

Stewart, G.R. (1994). An overview of the Mohave Desert and its herpetofauna. Pp. 55–69 *In* P.R. Brown and J.W. Wright (Eds.), Herpetology of the North American Deserts – Proceedings of a Symposium. Southwestern Herpetologists Society, Special Publication No. 5, Van Nuys, California.

Strickland, J.L., C.F. Smith, A.J. Mason, D.R. Schield, M. Borja, G. Castañeda-Gaytán, C.L. Spencer, L.L. Smith, A. Trápaga, N.M. Bouzid, G. Campillo-García, O.A. Flores-Villela, D. Antonio-Rangel, S.P. Mackessy, T.A. Castoe, D.R. Rokyta and C.L. Parkinson (2018). Evidence of divergent patterns of local selection driving venom variation in Mojave Rattlesnakes (*Crotalus scutulatus*). Scientific Reports 8:17622.

Sutherland, S.K., A.R. Coulter, and R.D. Harris (1979). Rationalisation of first-aid measures for elapid snakebite. Lancet 313(January 27, 1979):183–186.

Tennant, A. (1984). The Snakes of Texas. Texas Monthly Press, Austin, Texas.

Wilkinson, J.A., J.L. Glenn, R.C. Straight, and J.W. Sites, Jr. (1991). Distribution and generic variation in venom A and B populations of the Mojave rattlesnake (*Crotalus scutulatus scutulatus*) in Arizona. Herpetologica 47:54–68.

Wingert, W.A., and L. Chan (1988). Rattlesnake bites in southern California and rationale for recommended treatment. Western Journal of Medicine 148:37–44.

Wright, A.H., and A.A. Wright (1957). Handbook of Snakes of the United States and Canada, 2 vols. Cornell University Press, Ithaca, New York.

Wright, A.H., and A.A. Wright (1962). Handbook of Snakes of the United States and Canada, vol. 3, Bibliography. Cornell University Press, Ithaca, New York.

Wyeth Laboratories (1965). Antivenin (Crotalidae) Polyvalent (equine origin). (3rd ed.). Wyeth Laboratories, New York, New York.

Zancolli, G., T.G. Baker, A. Barlow, R.K. Bradley, J.J. Calvete, K.C. Carter, K. de Jager, J.B. Owens, J.F. Price, L. Sanz, A. Scholes-Higham, L. Shier, L. Wood, C.E. Wüster, and W. Wüster (2016). Is hybridization a source of adaptive venom variation in rattlesnakes? A test, using a *Crotalus scutulatus* x *viridis* hybrid zone in southwestern New Mexico. Toxins 8:188. doi:10.3390/toxins8060188

Zancolli, G., J.J. Calvete, M.D. Cardwell, H.W. Greene, W.K. Hayes, M.J. Hegarty, H.W. Hermann, A.T. Holycross, D.I. Lannutti, J.F. Mulley, L. Sanz, Z.D. Travis, J.R. Whorley, C.E. Wüster, and W. Wüster (2019). When one phenotype is not enough: divergent evolutionary trajectories govern venom variation in a widespread rattlesnake species. Proceedings of the Royal Society B 286: doi: http://dx.doi.org/10.1098/rspb. 2018.2735

Glossary

Antivenom (antivenin). Antibody molecules against specific snake venoms, raised in horses or sheep, then harvested, freeze dried, and used as an antidote for snakebite in humans.

Crotalinae. Pitvipers; the taxonomic subfamily of vipers with heat-sensing facial pits.

Disintegrins. A family of small proteins, some of which are released in pitviper venoms and implicated in allowing the snakes to find envenomated prey.

doi. Abbreviation for "digital object identifier," a unique alphanumeric link designed to be a persistent method to find a document on the Internet.

Ecdysis (shedding). The periodic process of replacing the corneal layer of skin in scaled reptiles.

Ecotone. The transition zone between different habitat types.

Efficacy. The ability to produce a desired or intended result.

Epoch. A unit of geological time; longer than an Age but shorter than a Period.

Etymology. The study of the origin of words and the way in which their meanings have changed throughout history.

Fasciotomy. A surgical procedure where a swollen limb is cut open to relieve pressure, commonly intended to preserve or reestablish blood flow in the limb.

LD_{50} test. A method in toxicology to determine the dosage of a toxin that kills 50% of test animals – the "Median Lethal Dose." It is used to compare lethality among different toxins.

Mass. The term used by scientists to describe the amount of matter in an object. For non-technical use, it is synonymous with "weight."

Metalloproteinase. A class of toxic components in viper venoms that typically causes hemorrhage, swelling, blister formation and necrosis at the site of the snakebite, as well as other local and systemic effects. Commonly abbreviated: SVMP (Snake Venom Metalloproteinase).

Mojave toxin. The potent pre-synaptic neurotoxin unique to Mohave rattlesnakes. It is spelled with a "j" because that is the spelling used by the researchers who first discovered, described, and named it.

Morphology. The branch of biology dealing with the form and structure of organisms.

MYA. Acronym for "million years ago."

Necrosis. Tissue death.

Nucleotide. Any of four molecular building blocks of DNA and RNA.

Phylogenetics. The study of Phylogeny, which is the evolutionary history of a taxonomic group of organisms.

Pleistocene. The first epoch of the Quaternary Period, occurring from about 2 MYA to 10,000 years ago. It falls between the Pliocene and Holocene Epochs.

Pliocene. The last epoch of the Tertiary Period, occurring from about 5 MYA to 2 MYA. It falls between the Miocene and Pleistocene Epochs.

Poison. In zoology, it is a toxic secretion produced by an organism without an accompanying delivery mechanism. Usual mode of delivery is ingestion or absorption. Compare to "venom."

Protease (Proteinase). An enzyme that destroys proteins and peptides (thus destroys tissue).

p-value (P-value). The statistical probability, expressed in decimal form, that a calculated result is due to chance or coincidence.

Shedding. See Ecdysis.

sp. Abbreviation for "species," usually meaning that multiple species of a genus are included; example: "Crotalus sp."

Supraocular scale. The large scale just above the eye of scaled reptiles.

Type location. The location from which a type specimen was collected.

Type specimen. The specimen from which the original description of a species (or genus, etc.) was produced.

Venom. A toxic secretion produced by an organism with an accompanying delivery mechanism. Usual mode of delivery is injection. Compare to "poison."

Venom-A. Mohave rattlesnake venom containing Mojave toxin without tissue-destroying metalloproteinase.

Venom-A+B. Mohave rattlesnake venom containing Mojave toxin and tissue-destroying metalloproteinase.

Venom-B. Mohave rattlesnake venom containing tissue-destroying metalproteinase without Mojave toxin.

Young-of-the-year. A juvenile rattlesnake in its first year of life.

About the Author

Mike Cardwell is a wildlife biologist who uses radiotelemetry to study the behavior and ecology of wild rattlesnakes. Fascinated with wildlife as a teenager in southern California's Mohave Desert, Mike got to know rattlesnakes as shy and intriguing animals that demanded respect due to their dangerous bite. At the same time, he became frustrated as he learned that Mohave rattlesnakes, in particular, were the subject of an incredible number of irrational myths that were passionately believed by most other people. As Mike attempted to educate himself in order to dispel the myths, he found that the species' behavior and natural history had not been well studied. Although much research had been carried out on Mohave rattlesnake venom, nobody had studied the private lives of the animals themselves–so he set out to do it.

He continued to pursue the scholarly study of rattlesnakes during a 32-year law enforcement career, including the first long-term field study of Mohave rattlesnakes, which was prominently featured in Animal Planet's "Venom ER" television series (2004). After retirement, Mike turned data from that study into a Master of Science degree from California State University Sacramento with a thesis on the behavior of Mohave rattlesnakes during drought. Among his many accomplishments along the way, he has documented the reproductive ecology of Mohave rattlesnakes (2008, Journal of Zoology), co-edited *The Biology of Rattlesnakes*, a 600-page compilation of research by 90 authors (2008, Loma Linda University Press), and served on the expert panel that revised snakebite treatment guidelines for the United States and Canada (2015, Wilderness & Environmental Medicine). Mike, along with colleagues at the

Smithsonian Institution and the Philadelphia Academy of Natural Sciences, re-described the "type specimen" of the Mohave rattlesnake, ending more than a hundred years of confusion (2013, *Proceedings of the Biological Society of Washington*).

Cardwell is now an adjunct researcher with San Diego State University, studying the behavior of wild rattlesnakes in the Sonoran Desert of southern Arizona. He lives in Tucson with his wife Denise.

Notes